DIY Résumé and Cover Letter Kit
Everything you need to create your own professional-quality résumé and cover letter

by Gabrielle Lichterman

Copyright ©2021 by Gabrielle Lichterman.
All rights reserved. This book, or parts thereof, may not be reproduced in any form without permission from the author; exceptions are made for brief excerpts used in published reviews.

Published by Happiness Upgrade Press
St. Petersburg, Florida, USA

ISBN-13: 978-1-7362353-1-7

DIY Résumé and Cover Letter Kit is designed to provide accurate and authoritative information with regard to the subject matter covered. It is sold with the understanding that the publisher is not engaged in rendering legal, accounting, or other professional advice. If legal advice or other expert assistance is required, the services of a competent professional should be sought.
—From a *Declaration of Principles* jointly adopted by a Committee of the American Bar Association and a Committee of Publishers and Associations

Résumés, cover letters, names, addresses and other personal details found in this guide and associated materials are fictitious. They are for demonstration purposes only.

Use of this book and its associated materials does not guarantee any offer of a job interview or employment.

CONTENTS

Preface iv
3 FREE BONUS GUIDES vi
Getting Started: Download Your Templates vii

Résumé DIY Guide

Résumé DIY Guide 1
Résumé-Writing Introduction 2
General Résumé-Writing Tips 3
Step-by-Step Résumé-Writing Instructions 8
    RÉSUMÉ STEP 1: Name 9
    RÉSUMÉ STEP 2: Professional Title 11
    RÉSUMÉ STEP 3: Contact Information 13
    RÉSUMÉ STEP 4: LinkedIn Profile 15
    RÉSUMÉ STEP 5: Highlights 18
    RÉSUMÉ STEP 6: Experience Title 23
    RÉSUMÉ STEP 7: Job Title 25
    RÉSUMÉ STEP 8: Dates of Employment 28
    RÉSUMÉ STEP 9: Company Name and Location 30
    RÉSUMÉ STEP 10: Responsibilities & Accomplishments ... 32
    RÉSUMÉ STEP 11: Notable Achievements 48
    RÉSUMÉ STEP 12: Education 53
    RÉSUMÉ STEP 13: Computer Skills 60
    RÉSUMÉ STEP 14: Optional Sections 62
    RÉSUMÉ STEP 15: Edit Your Résumé 70

Cover Letter DIY Guide

Cover Letter DIY Guide 72
Cover Letter-Writing Introduction 73
General Cover Letter-Writing Tips 74
Step-by-Step Cover Letter-Writing Instructions 77
    COVER LETTER STEP 1: Header 78
    COVER LETTER STEP 2: Date 79
    COVER LETTER STEP 3: Company Address 80
    COVER LETTER STEP 4: Greeting 83
    COVER LETTER STEP 5: Introductory Paragraph 85
    COVER LETTER STEP 6: Body of Your Letter 89
    COVER LETTER STEP 7: Closing 99
    COVER LETTER STEP 8: Signature 101
    COVER LETTER STEP 9: Edit Your Cover Letter 103

Résumé Examples 105
Cover Letter Examples 111
Troubleshooting the Editable, Preformatted Word Document 115
About Gabrielle Lichterman 117
More Information 118

Preface

You can write a professional-quality résumé and cover letter—really!

When someone wants a résumé and cover letter that lands them a job interview, they come to me. That's because I've been a **professional writer of résumés and cover letters** for more than 20 years. I'm also a longtime **personal finance journalist** who reports on trends in résumés, cover letters and hiring practices for major magazines. This makes me the expert who knows *exactly* what managers want to see when looking at employment applications.

While I enjoy writing résumés and cover letters for job-seekers, I truly don't believe you need to hire a professional like me to create them. **You can write your résumé and cover letter yourself**—even if you don't feel that you have strong writing skills. All you need is a little guidance about how to do it.

"If the only thing standing between you and your dream job is a résumé and cover letter, that shouldn't mean you have to pay someone a bundle of money to write them for you."

This is why I wrote the **DIY Résumé and Cover Letter Kit**. Whether you're looking for a new job, changing careers, starting out or returning to the workforce after a break, I want to help you get the position you want faster. Because if the **only thing standing between you and your dream job is a résumé and cover letter**, that shouldn't mean you have to pay someone a bundle of money to write them for you.

So, I created this simple-to-follow, step-by-step guide that shows you how to write a résumé and cover letter yourself. This DIY kit makes it **easy** because it...

- Breaks down instructions into **bite-sized steps**
- Gives you **lots of examples**
- Includes **editable, preformatted Word templates**

Bonus: I also share my best **insider tips**, favorite **tricks** and easy **shortcuts** that I've learned throughout my long career. They'll make your résumé and cover letter even more effective. You won't find these tips in any other book.

So, are you ready to take the first step toward creating your new résumé and cover letter? Here we go!

Gabrielle Lichterman
Author, DIY Résumé and Cover Letter Kit

3 FREE BONUS GUIDES

As a thank-you gift for purchasing my
DIY Résumé and Cover Letter Kit,
I'm giving you **3 FREE bonus guides**!

These guides give you easy tips that:
- ✓ Show you how to turn your social media account into **job magnets**,
- ✓ Help you find more **job openings**,
- ✓ Share secrets for acing your **job interview**

You get....

FREE BONUS GUIDE #1:
5 Ways to Use Social Media to Land a Job Faster

FREE BONUS GUIDE #2:
5 Ways (Other Than Indeed!) to Find a Job

FREE BONUS GUIDE #3:
5 Questions to Ask at Every Job Interview

Download your 3 FREE bonus guides:

GabrielleLichterman.com/DIYBonuses

Getting Started: Download Your Templates

Writing your résumé and cover letter is easy when you use the **DIY Résumé and Cover Letter Kit**.

To get started:

1. Download the editable, preformatted Microsoft Word **résumé and cover letter templates**:

GabrielleLichterman.com/DIYTemplates

2. Read the **General Résumé-Writing Tips**. Then, move on to the easy **Step-by-Step Résumé-Writing Instructions**.

3. Read the **General Cover Letter-Writing Tips**. Then, move on to the easy **Step-by-Step Cover Letter-Writing Instructions**.

4. Start **submitting** your new professional-quality résumé and cover letter to job openings!

Résumé DIY Guide

Everything you need to create your own professional-quality résumé

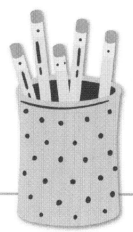

You get...
- ✓ Easy step-by-step instructions
- ✓ Editable, preformatted Word templates
- ✓ Insider tips and tricks from a pro

Résumé-Writing Introduction

Get your resume read...all the way through

When it comes to résumés, you've got to make a good impression **fast**!

That's because most hiring managers take just **a few seconds** to review a résumé before deciding whether or not to read further.

What's more, before a hiring manager even receives your résumé, it may go through an automated software program or get passed to a human resources staff member who scans it for **keywords and phrases** that describe your experience, education and other details related to the job you want. If they can't find these words, they won't even bother sending your résumé to the hiring manager. Instead, they'll simply move on to the next job candidate.

This is why it's critical for you to write a résumé that...

- ✓ Grabs the **attention** of the reader instantly
- ✓ Keeps them **reading**
- ✓ Helps them spot **keywords and phrases** quickly
- ✓ Makes your **skills and achievements** stand out
- ✓ Gets **moved up the chain** in the hiring process

The following **Step-by-Step Résumé Instructions** will help do all this. They quickly and easily guide you through every aspect of crafting the kind of résumé that makes you stand out and convinces hiring managers to invite you to a job interview.

LET'S GET STARTED:

1. Read the General Résumé-Writing Tips.

2. Move on to the easy Step-by-Step Résumé-Writing Instructions.

General Résumé-Writing Tips

Before you start writing your résumé, please review these general résumé-writing tips. They'll help make the whole process easier for you:

✓ **Backspace, then replace the text on the résumé template**

When adding your own text to the editable, preformatted Word résumé template, use the backspace button to remove each line of sample text in each section as you go through the step-by-step instructions. Backspacing will preserve the formatting (such as font, type size, bullets, indents, etc.) so the new text you add looks like the old text you're replacing.

If you try to select a block of text, then press delete, you may lose the formatting.

✓ **Undo if you need a do-over**

Made a mistake when changing the editable, preformatted Word résumé template? Not a problem. You can use the "undo" arrow (on the top left of your Word screen) or press Ctrl + z to make a correction. If you need to start over from scratch, simply download the editable, preformatted Word résumé template again. There is no limit to how many times you can download it.

✓ **Keep the résumé design simple**

I have deliberately created a résumé template with a simple, streamlined design. You will see many, many, *many* different résumé designs out there. And, chances are, when you begin using the template you downloaded for this kit, you'll get a prompt from your own Microsoft Word program asking if you want help creating a résumé. Then, it will offer you dozens of colorful, artistic designs to select.

However, it's important to keep the design of your résumé as simple as possible. That's because it makes it easier to read, which means the hiring manager will read *more* of it.

An added benefit: When you upload your résumé online when applying for a job, a simple style helps the company's job application software scan it. This makes the program more likely to pick up on keywords and phrases it's looking for that qualify you as a candidate.

✓ The <u>one time</u> it's okay to use graphics

The only time it's a benefit to use graphics, charts, colors, non-traditional fonts and other design elements in your résumé is when applying for a job that requires these skills, such as an art director or advertising designer.

For other positions, these kinds of flourishes tend to be a turn-off to hiring managers. That's because they send the message that you're trying to make up for a lack of experience and skills by overdesigning your résumé.

If you do use design elements because it's fitting for your career field, keep this in mind: Many companies require you to upload your résumé to a program on their website or a recruiter's website—and your information is then automatically plugged into an employment form. Any graphics you use can cause problems with what's entered into the fields, leading to missing text or text entered into the wrong places. So, you may want to create a traditional, graphics-free résumé first to upload for forms with autofill fields. Then, you can create a second résumé with graphics and upload that separately (which is commonly an option) to demonstrate your design skills.

✓ It's okay to have <u>more</u> than one page

There is a common belief that a résumé should never be longer than one page—but this is simply not true. If you have enough experience to fill one and a half pages, two pages or three pages, go ahead and include it.

However, do not throw in extra responsibilities, unrelated jobs or other unnecessary information just to fill out more pages. Sticking to the essentials helps the hiring manager focus on the most impactful details of your experience rather than get lost in a page full of "filler".

✓ Don't worry about having <u>less</u> than one page

If you're just starting out in the workforce, are a recent graduate or you've had only one or two jobs, don't worry about filling a page all the way to the bottom. It's okay to have less. Employers understand that you've got to start somewhere.

Plus, as you'll learn in the following step-by-step instructions, there are many items you can add to you résumé to fill it up that showcase your skills, such as volunteer work, internships and even your hobbies if they are related to the position you want.

✓ But, try to fix a "spillover"

If you've got a second or third page that has only one to five lines on it, try to shorten your résumé to get these lines to fit on the previous page. It makes your résumé look more professional and you look more detail-oriented to get rid of this "spillover".

To make room on the previous pages for these extra lines, delete job responsibilities that are least important and trim lists. You can also consider widening your right-hand margin. To widen the margin of your entire document, press Ctrl + a, then put your cursor on the Right Indent marker on the ruler and drag it to the right. (If you can't see your ruler in Word, click View on your top menu, then check "Ruler".) To widen the margin of just one section, left-click your mouse button and use your mouse to select a block of text, then drag the Right Indent marker to the right.

✓ Change your résumé with <u>every</u> job application

Yes, it's annoying, but every résumé you write needs to be tailored slightly to include keywords and phrases from each job ad, which will be different from ad to ad. That's because some employers may be looking more closely at your education and certifications while others may want to know more about your "hard" skills (such as what software you've been trained in) and still others may want to know more about your "soft" skills (meaning how you interact with team members, clients and customers).

Customizing your résumé to speak directly to each company's needs—rather than sending out the same general "cookie cutter" résumé to everyone—tells the hiring manager that you're passionate about their business specifically. And that makes you stand out from the crowd.

✓ What about sending your résumé <u>automatically</u>?

Indeed.com, LinkedIn.com and other career websites allow you to upload your résumé, then tap a button to automatically submit it for a position you find. It takes just seconds to do and you get your application in fast.

However, do *not* use this feature.

While it's okay to upload your résumé on these websites to allow recruiters *to find you*, using that one-button feature to submit a résumé for *a job you found* can actually end up costing you the interview.

Why? Most hiring managers (including those I've spoken with personally) are not fans of this feature. They see applicants who use it as lazy and unenthusiastic. What they prefer are applicants who take at least a few minutes to tailor their résumé for the job ad they're answering. That's because, as mentioned above, each company will be seeking slightly different skills or experience. By putting in that extra bit of effort to customize your résumé, you'll be making the best first impression—and you'll beat out applicants who used that "lazy" one-step résumé submission feature.

Plus: This automatic feature typically does not allow you to submit a cover letter with your résumé. As you'll see in the Cover Letter DIY Guide section, cover letters are critical to landing a job interview—and they need to be sent with nearly every application you submit.

✓ Do <u>not</u> include the following on your résumé...

While a résumé needs to contain certain words, phrases and sections to increase your chances of getting invited to a job interview, there are also certain words, phrases and sections to *avoid* including because they can lower your chances of getting that invitation. To make the best first impression, do not include...

- ✖ ***A "mission statement":*** For many years, job seekers included a mission statement at the top of their résumé that told potential employers their career goals. However, do not include one in your résumé since a mission statement is now considered outdated and unnecessary. In fact, including it makes you look as though you're not keeping up with the times, which can send the message that you also may not keep up with changes in your field.
- ✖ ***References:*** There is no need to include the names and contact information of supervisors and colleagues in your résumé. An employer will ask you for this information in an online submission form or after your job interview.
- ✖ ***"References available upon request":*** This line is not needed on your résumé since employers know you'll be providing them with references when they ask.
- ✖ ***Personal details:*** Avoid disclosing your marital status, if you currently have children, if you plan to have children and other personal details. Information about your private life can consciously or nonconsciously impact a hiring manager's decisions. You want to use your résumé to win over prospective employers with your experience, skills and accomplishments, which can help overcome any possible biases.
- ✖ ***Photo of yourself:*** The only time it's appropriate to include a photo of yourself in your job application is when applying for a position that requires it, for example, if you're seeking an on-camera media position.

Step-by-Step Résumé-Writing Instructions

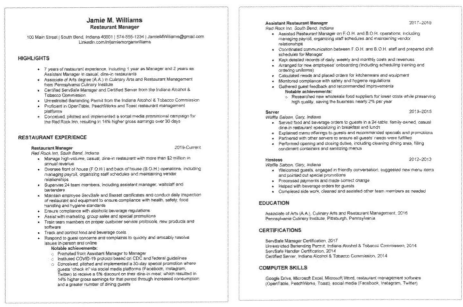

Above is what your résumé will end up looking like by the time you're finished.

All you have to do is follow the simple **Step-by-Step Résumé-Writing Instructions** that follow. They'll show you how to list your job experience, education, internships, volunteer positions, military background and/or achievements in ways that impress hiring managers and keep them reading.

Get started:

Download the editable, preformatted Microsoft Word résumé template:

GabrielleLichterman.com/DIYTemplates

RÉSUMÉ STEP 1: Name

Place your name front and center. Put your name in the **center** at the top of the page. A name that pops out conveys self-assurance.

Make it big. Put your name in a slightly **bigger size type** than the rest of the text on this page. It's 18-point in the template you've downloaded for this kit, but you can change the size if you want.

Be bold. Put your name in **bold** to further help it stand out.

Which name to use? If you go by **more than one name or have changed names** (for example, for different career fields, due to marriage or divorce, an author's pseudonym, a stage name, gender affirmation, etc.), use the name that is most appropriate for your current situation or for the job to which you're applying. However, if the name you use on LinkedIn or documents that an employer will likely see before they hire you is different than the one you use on your résumé, you may want to **briefly explain** in your cover letter why there's a difference to avoid confusion.

Examples:

If you review my Cosmetology license, please keep in mind that it was filed with my former married name, Arden Moore.

I wrote 3 eBooks about high impact LED lighting under my professional pen name, Riley Barker, which were published by LightAll Press.

PRO TIP

Consider adding a middle initial to your name. Middle initials on résumés—such as Jamie M. Williams—can make you appear smarter and more competent to hiring managers, according to a study in the *European Journal of Social Psychology*. Why? People are used to seeing middle initials in formal contexts, for example, on diplomas. So, they automatically associate them with greater intelligence.[1]

---

[1] Wijnand A. P. van Tilburg, Eric R. Igou, "The impact of middle names: Middle name initials enhance evaluations of intellectual performance," *European Journal of Social Psychology*, 44 (2014): 400-411.

RÉSUMÉ STEP 2:
Professional Title

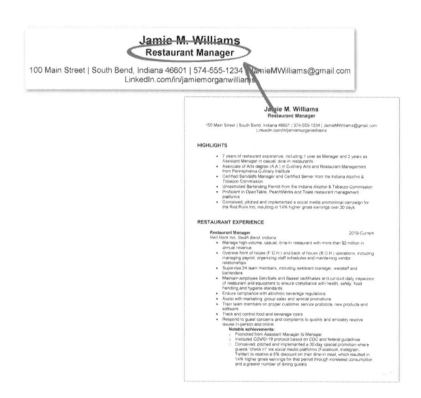

Match it up. Centered underneath your name, type your professional title. This is the job you have now or have had in the past. Your professional title will typically **match the title of the position** for which you're applying.

Including a professional title on your résumé ensures that the company's software program or human resources department picks up on one of the most important keywords in your résumé—the **name of the position** that's available.

It also reinforces to the hiring manager who's selecting candidates that you're a **perfect fit** for the job.

Examples:

Accountant
Editor and Copywriter
Engineer
Graphic Designer
Registered Nurse
Restaurant Manager
Social Media Coordinator
Teacher

Or use a general title. Are you applying for a job you haven't yet held? For example, are you looking to **climb your career ladder** and there's an opening for a manager, but you've only gotten to the point of assistant manager in the past? Or are you **changing careers**, say, from accountant to teacher? In these cases, use **general terms** that sum up the profession you're in or the one you're entering.

Examples:

Accounting
Editing and Copywriting
Engineering
Graphic Design
Nursing
Restaurant Management
Social Media Coordination
Teaching

RÉSUMÉ STEP 3:
Contact Information

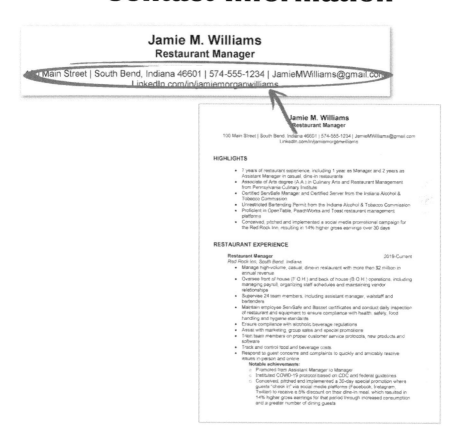

Skip a line, then add your contact information. Place your contact details underneath your job title. In the editable, preformatted Word résumé template, this information is placed two lines below your professional title, so there's **a line skipped between**. This extra space makes it easier to read.

Add your details. Include your **mailing address**, **phone number** and **email address**.

Do not bother adding two phone numbers (such as a landline and mobile phone) since it's just clutter. Include just **one phone number** that's best for reaching you.

Make your email professional. Use an email address that is **yourname@gmail.com**.

Example:

JamieMWilliams@gmail.com

You can also use your **own domain** if you have one for your name (such as Jamie@JamieWilliams.com) or business (such as Jamie@TopNotchDesigns.com).

Any other kind of email address can appear **unprofessional**, such as from other email providers (for example, Yahoo.com) or using random letters, words, characters or numbers (such as DayTripper321@gmail.com).

Don't have a Gmail account yet? Gmail is a **free** email service. You can sign up at Accounts.Google.com/signup.

If your name is already taken in Gmail, use a **variation**, such as "JMWilliams@gmail.com".

RÉSUMÉ STEP 4:
LinkedIn Profile

Place your LinkedIn URL right below. If you have a LinkedIn profile, include its URL address **directly underneath** your contact information. This would be: LinkedIn.com/in/yourprofilename.

Name your link. Before you type your LinkedIn URL, make sure it has been **personalized to your name**—meaning it's not the default random letters and numbers you were given when you first signed up. For example, "Jamie Morgan Williams" would be Linkedin.com/in/jamiemorganwilliams.

To change your LinkedIn profile URL to your name:

- Visit LinkedIn.com and log in to your account
- Click your photo on the top right menu, click "Settings & Privacy" in the dropdown menu
- Click "Visibility" in the left-hand menu
- Click "Change" in the "Edit your public profile" section
- Click the blue pencil in the "Edit your custom URL" section, which is on the upper right-hand side of the page
- Type your name
- Click Save
- If that name is taken, try a variation, such as including your middle initial, then save

Note: When you change your LinkedIn URL address, the **previous link will no longer work**. So, if you've included the old link in other documents (for example, job applications you're still waiting to hear about), you may want to consider starting a second LinkedIn account that contains the same information as the old one. This way, everyone who got the link to your original account can still access it.

Make it match. If you include your LinkedIn account on your résumé, make sure that all the information in your LinkedIn profile (dates of employment, job titles, responsibilities, etc.) **match what you put in your résumé**. Many hiring managers look at LinkedIn profiles to confirm that the information they read on your résumé is accurate.

Set it to be seen. If you're including your LinkedIn URL on your résumé, you'll need to set your profile to be seen by others—either LinkedIn members or everyone, which includes LinkedIn members and non-members. This allows hiring managers and others involved in the recruiting process to **see the information** on your LinkedIn page.

If you're concerned about **privacy**, choose the "All LinkedIn members" option. This prevents anyone who doesn't have a

LinkedIn account from seeing your information, for example, if someone is searching you online. Most hiring managers will have a LinkedIn account, so they'll be able to access it. If privacy is not a concern, select the "Public" option, which can be seen by anyone.

To change your LinkedIn visibility settings:

- Visit LinkedIn.com and log in to your account
- Click your photo on the top right menu, then "Settings & Privacy" in the dropdown menu
- Click "Visibility" in the left-hand menu
- Click "Change" in the "Edit your public profile" section
- Scroll down to the "Your Profile's Public Visibility" section on the right-hand side, then make sure the button is in the "on" position.
- If it says "off", tap it with your cursor to turn it on, then it will be visible to the public
- Select "Basic", then choose which viewing option you prefer: "All LinkedIn members" or "Public"

Don't have a LinkedIn account yet? You can sign up for **free** at LinkedIn.com. This website offers add-on options for a fee, but you do not have to pay to use its basic services.

RÉSUMÉ STEP 5: Highlights

HIGHLIGHTS

- 7 years of restaurant experience, including 1 year as Manager and 2 years as Assistant Manager in casual, dine-in restaurants
- Associate of Arts degree (A.A.) in Culinary Arts and Restaurant Management from Pennsylvania Culinary Institute
- Certified ServSafe Manager and Certified Server from the Indiana Alcohol & Tobacco Commission
- Unrestricted Bartending Permit from the Indiana Alcohol & Tobacco Commission
- Proficient in OpenTable, PeachWorks and Toast restaurant management platforms
- Conceived, pitched and implemented a social media promotional campaign for the Red Rock Inn, resulting in 14% higher gross earnings over 30 days

What are Highlights?

The "Highlights" section is a **must-have** for every résumé. It's so vital, in fact, that 4 in 10 senior managers said in a survey that including it can make you more likely to get the job.[1] That's because this section helps hiring personnel spot key aspects of your qualifications in an instant.

---

[1] RH-US.mediaroom.com/2020-01-08-Survey-Reveals-Job-Search-Trends-For-2020

So, what is your Highlights section? It's a short list (about 4 to 6 items) at the very top of your résumé of the **most important and outstanding aspects** of your experience, skills, accomplishments, education, certifications, achievements, honors and/or other vital details related to the job you want.

It also includes **keywords and phrases** taken directly from the job ad you're answering. These are words hiring managers specifically look for to figure out if you have the requirements for the position. They're also what résumé-scanning software programs search for to figure out if your application should be moved up the hiring chain and be shown to an actual human.

Fortunately, the Highlights section is simple to write. The following tips will guide you and answer questions you may have:

Put it at the top. Your Highlights section is placed at the top of your résumé right under your name and contact information. It's the **first thing** you want hiring managers to see.

Write a list of 4 to 6 items. To create your Highlights section, write a list of **four to six important details** that you want potential employers to know about you. Try to include keywords and phrases that are found in the job ad you're responding to.

Following are some suggestions to include in your Highlights list:

- **Years:** Mention how many years you've been in your field, you've held specific positions and/or you've been at a prestigious employer. Years are great to include in your Highlights list because they're easy to understand and **tell your professional history in an instant**.

    Examples:

    7 years of restaurant experience, including 3 years as Assistant Manager

- **Educational degree:** If the position requires a specific degree (such as a B.A., B.B.A., B.S., D.O., Ed.D., M.D., M.S.W., N.P., Ph.D., Psy.D., R.D. or R.N.), include it in this section. Write out the **degree name fully** and also include its **abbreviation** in parentheses. This ensures your degree is detected by a company's résumé-scanning software. Include what subject your degree is in if it's related to your field.

    Also smart: Include the word **"degree"** in case the software scans for it. And, include any notable educational achievement, such as *magna cum laude*.

    You can include your **school name** as well, especially if you feel it will help you stand out, for example, because it's a prestigious school, local institution or has ties to the company for which you want to work.

    Examples:

    Master of Social Work (M.S.W.) degree from Indiana University

    Bachelor of Science (B.S.) degree in Environmental Science, magna cum laude, from Boston University

- **Special training:** Do you have a trade license? Did you get a certification? Are you trained on a trade-specific software? If you have **extra training** that is related to the job opening, include it in your Highlight sections.

    As with degrees, type out the **full name** of what you're trained in, then also include its **abbreviation** (if it has one) in parentheses next to the name to ensure that scanning software detects it.

Examples:

Certified Public Accountant (C.P.A.) licensed by the Florida Board of Accountancy

New York City High Pressure Boiler Operating Engineer License

Certified in Cardiopulmonary Resuscitation (C.P.R.) from Red Cross

- **Notable accomplishments:** Have you done anything in your current or past jobs that makes you **stand out**? For example, did you pitch a big project that was successfully implemented? Did you increase your company's revenue? Were you selected for a prestigious task? Include one or two of the most impressive accomplishments that show your passion for the industry and motivation to help the company for which you work succeed.

    Examples:

    Conceived, pitched and implemented Childtime Clothing's first online social media campaign that resulted in 7% higher profits in the first quarter

    Featured speaker at the 2020 Consumer Electronics Show (C.E.S.) in Las Vegas, Nevada

Customize this list. When applying for each job, add and subtract **keywords, phrases and pieces of information** based on the requirements listed in the posting. For example, some companies emphasize that they're looking for someone with specific training and certifications while others prefer a certain amount of job experience.

Use short phrases. Stick to short, **to-the-point facts**. You do not need full sentences in this section. Ideally, each line is one phrase that talks about one key experience or a related group of key experiences.

Examples:

3 years as Assistant Supervisor of Appliance Repairs at Exceptional Hi-Tech Appliance Repair in Gary, Indiana

5 years as an Appliance Repair Technician diagnosing and repairing consumer appliances that span a wide range of manufacturers, including General Electric, Maytag and Whirlpool

Avoid punctuation. End each line **without** a period. Since these are phrases, they do not need punctuation.

Skip generic statements. The Highlights section is where you show off **specific achievements, certifications and experience**. Avoid generic descriptions, such as "detail-oriented", "excellent people skills" and "highly motivated". These kinds of empty phrases turn off hiring managers because they don't share anything concrete about your job skills. Including precise details gives them a clear picture of what makes you perfect for this position.

PRO TIP

Come back to this section again at the end. You may find it helpful to return to your Highlights list once you've filled out the rest of your résumé. Why? As you go through all the other sections, it might jog your memory of important job responsibilities, notable achievements and other key facets of your experience that you hadn't added to your Highlights, but are worth including.

RÉSUMÉ STEP 6:
Experience Title

What is your Experience Title?

This is a short phrase you'll be using to **describe all the job experience** you're listing on your résumé. It's placed right above your list of current and previous positions. It's a little like a book title—it sums up what the subject of the content is about for the reader.

Use your career field's name. If you **have experience that's related** to the job you're seeking, type the name of your career field and the word "experience". This reinforces to hiring managers that you've worked in positions similar to jobs that they're looking to fill.

Examples:

RESTAURANT EXPERIENCE

MARKETING EXPERIENCE

TEACHING EXPERIENCE

Or use a general title. If you **do not have experience** related to the job you're seeking or you have a wide mix of jobs that are not directly related to each other, then type: PROFESSIONAL EXPERIENCE.

You can **explain in your cover letter** how your unrelated experience or newly adopted skills, education or certifications make you qualified for the job you want.

If you have two career paths. If you have a solid work history with **two types of job experience**, separate them into their own categories and list the related jobs in each category. You would usually do this in special circumstances, such as if you're trying to switch from one field to another or explain job gaps in one field.

Examples:

PSYCHOTHERAPY EXPERIENCE
TEACHING EXPERIENCE

CONTRACT LAW EXPERIENCE
NON-PROFIT CONSULTING EXPERIENCE

RÉSUMÉ STEP 7:
Job Title

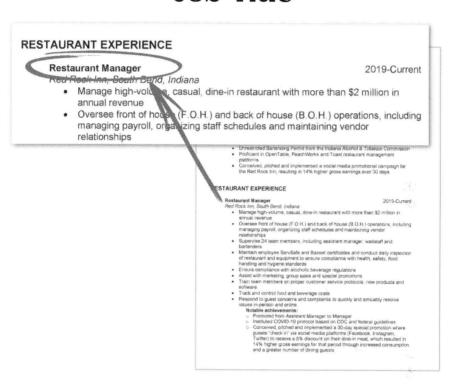

Start with your latest job. Your list of job experiences in your résumé starts with your **current or most recent** position. Then, you work your way backward. So, the first job title you type will be the position you currently hold or the one you most recently held.

Below it you'll include the job you held **right before your most recent or current job**. Below it goes the job you held before that one. Then, below it goes the job you held before that. And so on.

Format it right. Put the **first letter of each word** in your job title in capital letters.

Examples:

Restaurant Manager

Emergency Nurse

Director of Activities

Make it stand out. Put the job title in **bold**.

Match your LinkedIn profile. If you have a LinkedIn profile or a bio elsewhere online, be sure that your **job title matches** what you write on your résumé. Many employers will check to confirm the information they find on websites is similar to the résumé in their hand.

If you're a gig worker. If you work or have worked as a **freelancer** (or "gig" worker or contractor) for one or more clients, your job title will be "Freelance" and the name of the job you do.

Examples:

Freelance Editor

Freelance Web Designer

Include the right number of jobs. If you have more than 20 years of work experience or fewer than 5 years of work experience, you may wonder if you're putting **too much or too little** information on your résumé. Here's a quick rundown of what to do in both cases:

- **If you have lots of work experience:** Include only the jobs that are related to the position for which you're applying and that you've held **longer than one year**.
  You can include internships, volunteer positions, temporary positions and short-term assignments that are shorter than one year if they are **related to your field** and

show **some kind of benefit**. One example: an internship that gave you more experience with a certain software program.

- **If you do not have a lot of work experience:** Include **internships and volunteer positions** in your list of jobs. Then, try to figure out which responsibilities and skills from these experiences relate to the job you're seeking. One example: If you posted photos of adoptable dogs and cats on social media for a pet adoption organization, these are skills that you'd also use for an online content creator position.

You can also list **hobbies** in your résumé under work experience as long as they directly relate to your professional field. For example, if you want to apply to be a web designer at a company, you can include "Freelance web designer" in your job experience, then include samples of websites you've designed for friends and family, describe the programs you use to design them and add other details as you would with any other job. (We'll get more into the details in the following chapters.)

RÉSUMÉ STEP 8:
Dates of Employment

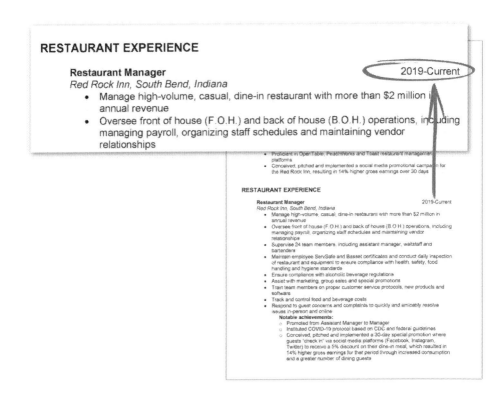

Place it right. The length of time you spent at each job goes on the **right-hand side** of your job title. This makes it easy for the reader to spot.

Note the length in years. If your job experience lasted **longer than one year**, type the years you worked at this position. Type "Current" if you're still employed. In many cases, the specific starting and ending months are not needed on a résumé for long-held positions.

Examples:

2017-Current

2017-2020

Add the month for these reasons: You'll need to add the month you started and (if applicable) ended a job if...

- You're asked for **specific start and end dates**
- Your experience was **under one year**
- There is a specific **reason for the dates related to the job**, for example, it was a one-semester internship, you had a short-term contract or the work was seasonal

Examples:

June 2017-August 2017

January 2015-November 2015

RÉSUMÉ STEP 9:
Company Name and Location

Add the business name. Under your job title, type the **name** of the company, institution, organization, school, non-profit group, etc., where you work now or where you have worked in the past.

Add the region. Next to that, type its **general location**. Type out the full name of the city, state or region. Do not use abbreviations. You do not need a full street address or zip code. This simply gives the reader an idea of where your previous job was located.

Examples:

Green Mountain Café, Portland, Oregon

Queen Anne Hospital, London, United Kingdom

Were you a remote worker who was an employee? If you worked remotely for a specific company and were considered an **employee** (not a contractor), type the name of the company and the location of its headquarters or the branch office with which you're affiliated. In the job's description, you can state that you worked remotely.

Examples:

Oregon Parks and Recreation, Salem, Oregon

Brightwater Publishing, Camberwell, Australia

Were you a remote worker who was a contractor? If you worked remotely for a specific company, but it was officially as a **contractor or freelancer** and not an "employee", type the name of the company, the word "Remote", and the location where you're typically doing your work (such as your home or personal office).

Examples:

Belle Aire Museum, Remote, Chicago, Illinois

Barkley Investments, Remote, Ithaca, New York

RÉSUMÉ STEP 10: Responsibilities & Accomplishments

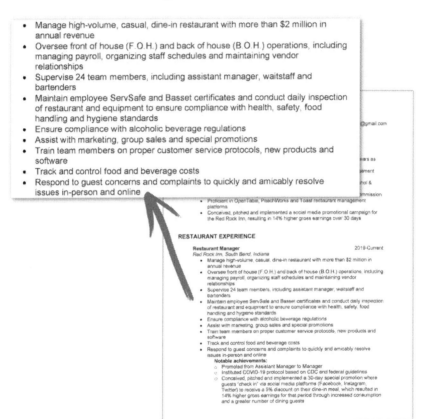

What are your Responsibilities & Accomplishments?

Underneath the company name and location, write a bulleted list of **responsibilities and accomplishments** you had for each job you include in your résumé.

These are just like the items you include in your Highlights section at the top—**short, to-the-point facts**. These are not full sentences. There are no periods at the end of each line.

This section can be the most challenging part of writing a résumé for many people, so follow these **simple steps** to make it easier:

Write all tasks first. Open a new document in Word or grab a notebook and open up to a fresh page. Then, for each job you held, write a **complete list** of all the tasks you did and accomplishments you achieved. Also include computer software programs, professional websites and apps that you've used in your jobs.

For this list, don't worry about grammar, punctuation, spelling or writing it correctly. You simply want to remember everything you did so you **have it on hand to refer to**.

Need help remembering all you did and accomplished at each job? Go to the end of this chapter for a list of **questions to ask yourself** to help jog your memory so you don't miss anything important.

Search a job ad for keywords and phrases. To get your first résumé written (the basic one you'll change slightly every time you apply for a job opening), pick one job ad from all the open positions that interest you right now. Then, look for keywords and phrases the employer uses to **describe the qualifications they're looking for** (and that you presumably have). It's important to include exact keywords and phrases in your bulleted lists of responsibilities and accomplishments in your résumé. By matching the language the company uses in its ad, your application has a greater chance of being selected by their résumé-scanning software or moved up the chain by Human Resources.

The keywords and phrases will need to be **changed to match** those used by each company in their job ad. They will likely vary slightly from ad to ad. But, for now, start with just the one ad so you can build your basic résumé. Then, you can tweak it later for each application.

Trim your list. Once you have your complete list of responsibilities and accomplishments as well as keywords and phrases from the job ad you selected, it's time to **choose which items and words** will go into this section of your résumé.

Aim for a bulleted list of between **5 to 12** responsibilities and accomplishments for each job you have on your résumé.

Include responsibilities and accomplishments that the **employer wants to see most** based on what's in their job ad.

And include those that **show off** your skills and accomplishments.

Note: You may have **fewer** items to include in your bulleted list for some jobs because they were short-term positions or had limited tasks. And some jobs may require you to list **more** items because they were long-term positions or had a wider variety of tasks. It's okay if they don't fit within the 5 to 12 guideline. Use your best judgment.

However, if you had *dozens* of responsibilities at your job, do not include all of them. In cases when you did a far greater number of tasks, hiring managers prefer to read only about the **most important responsibilities** and those that **relate to the position** to which you are applying.

Organize your bulleted list. There's a **specific order** when it comes to listing your responsibilities and achievements. Here's a guide to what to put first, then what goes after.

- **First bulleted item: General summary.** The first item that goes in your bulleted list is a **general summary of the primary responsibility** you had at the company or for your business. Also, describe the company, for example, its size, location, annual revenue, whether it's historic or it's somehow notable.

    Examples:

    Assisted the Director of Development in fundraising efforts for a historic 104-year-old social service agency that caters to the needs of disadvantaged, immigrant and senior populations living in New York City's Lower East Side

Oversaw all cash management and investment-related functions for a mid-sized property and casualty insurance company in Denver, Colorado

- **Next bulleted items: Important tasks go first.** List the responsibilities and accomplishments you add after the first line in order of **how important they are according to the job ad.** Place the most important, impressive and job ad-related items in the second, third and fourth lines (under the general summary). The less important the item is, the lower it goes on the list.

  If computer programs, websites or apps are required for the job you want, include them in this list in the order of **how important the role is** that they play in the position. If they play a big role, list them up top. If they play a smaller role, list them toward the bottom.

Format each line. There are specific ways to format your bulleted list of responsibilities and achievements that make it **easier for hiring managers to read**. They also save time and space. They are:

- **Start most lines with an action verb.** These are words that **demonstrate actions you took** at your jobs, such as: "Organized", "Distributed" and "Coordinated".

  When writing about a job you **currently have**, you'll write in the present tense (such as "Organize", "Distribute" and "Coordinate").

  When writing about **past jobs**, you'll write in the past tense (such as "Organized", "Distributed" and "Coordinated").

Examples:

Pitch, design and implement fundraising efforts, such as direct mail campaigns, speaking engagements and events

Prepared monthly cash flow analysis

- **But not every line gets an action verb.** There are some **exceptions** where you do not start a line with an action verb, for example, when you have a job responsibility that was more of a role you held or when you're making a list. In these cases, simply state the facts you want to share.

    Examples:

    Development editor for a series of baking guides

    Online tutoring classes covered a wide range of topics, including math, science and history

- **Skip the "I".** Avoid starting lines with the word "I" since it's **understood** that you're the person who performed these functions.

- **Forget the period.** The items in your list of responsibilities and accomplishments are phrases—which means they are **not complete sentences**, so there is no period at the end of each line.

- **Capitalize the first word.** After the bullet, the **first letter of the first word** is uppercase, for example, "Pitched creative ideas".

- **Put lists of examples in order.** When listing numerous examples in one line (for instance, all the software programs you use or all the responsibilities you have for a task), arrange them either in **alphabetical** order or in order of **importance** for the field you're in. You can decide which type of order is best for your résumé.

Examples:

Used Adobe Illustrator, Adobe Photoshop, Microsoft Excel and Microsoft Word on a regular basis

Promoted store loyalty program, credit card offers and sales to customers while assisting them at the register

Start each line differently. It's best to start each line in your bulleted list with a different word. This makes it more **interesting for the readers**, which encourages them to keep reading. In instances when you have two or more responsibilities that are similar, try your best to use different first words to explain them.

Example:

Assist the Store Manager in day-to-day tasks, workflow, team-building, promotional displays, customer inquiries and phone calls

Support the Store Manager in special projects by providing performance analysis and reporting direct feedback from customers

Keep each line simple. People have **short attentions spans**, so they'll lose focus if they have to slog through long lines with lots of details. It's better to…

- **Use plain language.** Many people think they need to add flourishy words to a résumé to make it look better. But, unnecessary big words just **slow down readers**. For instance, many people write the word "utilize" (such as, *"Utilize Microsoft Excel to create custom spreadsheets"*) when "use" would be better since it's a shorter word that's far easier to read *("Use Microsoft Excel to create custom spreadsheets"*).

- **Stick to one idea per line.** While you can list more than one responsibility in a single line, try to **group them by topic** to make it easier for the reader to digest.

  Examples:

  Conceived, pitched, organized, implemented and supervised the company's first social media campaign

  Analyzed rates for click-through, lead-to-conversion and return-on-investment throughout the lifetime of the social media campaign to measure effectiveness

Use numbers when you can. Hiring managers love numbers because they **quickly relay important information** about your experience. For example, you can include the number of years you've worked in a position, how much work product you produced, the size of a company based on its assets, how much revenue a project you led earned or how many hours you saved your department because of a more efficient system you created.

When writing a number to describe achievements, tasks, a company's size, etc., use the **numeric version** (1, 2, 3, etc.) rather than writing it out alphabetically since this makes a bigger impact on the reader.

Examples:

Pitched, researched and wrote 15 to 20 articles per month for Healthline.com, the second-largest consumer *health website with an annual revenue of $30 million Manage working capital for a private hospital system with 14 facilities and an over $1 Billion operating budget to ensure liquidity for day-to-day operations*

If you are applying for a **writing and/or editing position**, check which editing style the company uses for numbers (such as Chicago Manual of Style or Associated Press Stylebook), then follow that model.

Avoid generic statements. Hiring managers don't want to read empty phrases, such as "detail-oriented", "excellent people skills", "team player" or "highly motivated". They want you to **show that you have these kinds of traits** through your responsibilities and accomplishments.

Examples:

SHOWS YOU'RE DETAIL-ORIENTED:
Wrote, copyedited and proofread an extensive variety of marketing and communications materials including email campaigns, video scripts, social media posts and newsletters

SHOWS YOU HAVE EXCELLENT PEOPLE SKILLS:
Assisted with conflict resolution using the company's 12-step resolution guideline to ensure customer satisfaction

SHOWS YOU'RE A TEAM PLAYER:
Worked hand-in-hand with graphic designers and web developers to create engaging online content

SHOWS YOU'RE HIGHLY MOTIVATED:
Pitched a weekly team member brainstorming session, which was implemented and resulted in 3 employee-led projects being adopted within the first 9 months

Held more than one position at the same job? If you got promoted, moved to a different department or took on another job title at a single place of employment (for example, you were promoted from assistant manager to manager at the same restaurant), you may be wondering if you write them as separate jobs. Well, **that depends**. Here's the general rule to follow:

If the **job duties were largely different** (it's okay if there's some overlap), then you write each role on your résumé separately as different jobs. You do not have to repeat the description of the employer in your "General Summary" line. (For more about your General Summary, scroll up to the "Organize Your Bulleted List" tip.)

Example:

Server 2013–2015
Waffle Saloon, Gary, Indiana
- *Served food and beverage orders to guests in a 24-table, family-owned, casual dine-in restaurant*
- *Performed opening and closing duties, including cleaning dining area, filling condiment containers and sanitizing*

Hostess 2012–2013
Waffle Saloon, Gary, Indiana
- *Welcomed guests and suggested new menu items*
- *Processed payments and made correct change*

But, if the **job duties were largely the same** (it's okay if there are a few differences), then you write them as one job on your résumé and include each different job title, plus the years you held that title next to it.

Example:

Associate Editor 2018-2020
Assistant Editor 2016-2018
Luxe Designers, Boston, Massachusetts

- *Wrote and edited copy for websites and print catalogues for a high-end fashion designer specializing in women's apparel and handbags*

Fill in gaps with alternative "jobs". Changing careers, new to the workforce, a recent graduate or have gaps in your work history? You have **options** for filling in professional experience on your résumé:

- **Include volunteer positions.** Write about them just as you would write about a traditional job—with a job title, dates, company name and list of responsibilities and accomplishments. Indicate it was a volunteer position in your job title (for example, "Volunteer Social Media Coordinator") or bulleted list (such as "Managed the social media account of a small non-profit art gallery as a volunteer"). Try to include skills and responsibilities that tie to the job you're seeking. Or explain how this experience relates to the job in your cover letter.

- **Include internships.** Write about them just as you would write about a traditional job—with a job title, dates, company name and list of responsibilities and accomplishments. Indicate it was an internship position in your job title (for example, "Social Media Coordinator Intern") or bulleted list ("Managed the social media account of a small non-profit art gallery during a 4-month intern program"). Try to include skills and responsibilities that tie to the job you're currently seeking. Or explain how this experience relates to the position to you want in your cover letter.

- **Include temporary or short-term positions.** Even jobs that you've held less than one year can demonstrate abilities and skills that relate to the job you want. Employers understand that some positions are temporary or short-term, such as seasonal positions, or that circumstances could cut a job short, for example if you moved to a new city or a company closed.

- **Include side gigs.** Do you have an Etsy storefront? Do website design as a freelancer? You can write about your side gig just like you would a traditional job. When possible, try to relate your experiences with it to the position to which you're applying.

Questions to Ask Yourself

Need help remembering all you did and accomplished? Interview yourself! Asking yourself the following questions for each position you include in your résumé will help jog your memory so you can add more detail and important information:

- What was the most important function or collection of functions you performed in your position?

- Did you supervise people? If so, how many?

- Did you teach, train or mentor employees or interns? If so, how many and what did you teach them?

- Did you oversee anyone else's work to ensure accuracy? For example, did you review, correct, edit or amend work by another employee (including your supervisor or company owner) or department?

- As part of your regular job duties, did you lead, coordinate or manage any group, team, committee or project?

- As part of your regular job duties, did you participate in a group, team, committee or project—and did you play a key role in it? For example, were you a member of the company recruitment team? Or did you belong to the fundraising committee and were responsible for taking notes?

- Were you responsible for updating anything for the company? For example, did you update the daily restaurant menu board, make changes on the company website or reconcile company bank records?

- Were you responsible for scheduling anything? For example, did you schedule work shifts, building maintenance or employee training?

- As part of your regular job duties, were you one of the spokespeople who represented the company? For example, did you speak at conferences, teach classes, manage booths, give tours, travel or get interviewed by the media?

- Did you assist or provide support to other employees or departments?

- Did you step in and assume the duties of another employee or department in their absence? For example, were you the Acting Director when your supervisor was on leave? Were you given managerial duties to perform while the Manager was traveling?

- Did you act as a liaison (link) between employees, contractors, departments or other people related to your company or job?

- Did you initiate, plan, schedule and/or lead virtual or in-person meetings?

- Did you delegate responsibilities to others? For example, did you divvy up tasks between employees or departments for day-to-day duties? Or did you assign and coordinate tasks to others during special events, such as your company's annual fundraiser?

- Were there any weekly, bi-weekly, monthly, bi-monthly, quarterly, annual or bi-annual tasks you did that were important? For example, were you responsible for taking monthly inventory or creating year-end reports?

Examples of Responsibilities and Accomplishments

Want more inspiration? Below are examples of responsibilities and accomplishments to help spur your imagination as you craft your own bulleted lists:

Hired and supervised a team of 14 servers and 2 bartenders

Identified, recommended and implemented cash management strategies to enhance existing processes for internal customers

Collaborated with health professionals, such as psychiatrists and primary care physicians, on patient treatment

Maintained equipment, including conveyer systems, air handlers, filter changes and lighting

Provided tax advice, tax return review and preparation to more than 400 TurboTax customers

Assumed managerial duties in Chief Engineer's absence, including meeting with contractors, scheduling workloads and delegating tasks

Coordinated art and editorial departments, acted as a liaison between editors and publisher and arranged layouts

Conceived, designed and implemented 14 social media campaigns on Facebook and Instagram

Trained 4 sales associates on providing stellar customer service, creating a welcoming store atmosphere and taking accurate inventory

Action Verb Examples

Acted	Coordinated	Followed	Launched
Acquired	Corrected	Formatted	Led
Administered	Crafted	Formed	Listed
Adopted	Created	Formulated	Listened
Advanced	Cultivated	Fostered	Maintained
Aggregated	De-escalated	Found	Managed
Alerted	Decided	Founded	Mediated
Allocated	Decorated	Furnished	Mentored
Altered	Decreased	Galvanized	Met
Amended	Delegated	Gathered	Negotiated
Analyzed	Deleted	Gauged	Notified
Announced	Delivered	Generated	Observed
Answered	Designed	Graded	Offered
Arranged	Developed	Granted	Orchestrated
Assembled	Directed	Handled	Ordered
Assessed	Dispersed	Helped	Organized
Assisted	Disseminated	Hired	Outlined
Backed up	Distributed	Identified	Overhauled
Bid	Downloaded	Impacted	Oversaw
Brainstormed	Earned	Implemented	Performed
Built	Edited	Improved	Persuaded
Calculated	Encouraged	Incorporated	Photographed
Chose	Engaged	Increased	Picked
Coached	Enhanced	Initiated	Pinpointed
Collaborated	Ensured	Inputted	Pitched
Collected	Established	Instituted	Placed
Communicated	Estimated	Instructed	Planned
Compared	Evaluated	Integrated	Posted
Completed	Exceeded	Interpreted	Predicted
Conceived	Expanded	Interviewed	Prepared
Conducted	Filed	Introduced	Presented
Consulted	Filled	Investigated	Produced
Contacted	Filmed	Judged	Projected
Cooperated	Flagged	Kept	Provided

Published	Resolved	Spent	Tracked
Purchased	Reviewed	Spoke	Trained
Ran	Revised	Stacked	Transformed
Read	Revitalized	Stocked	Transitioned
Received	Sanitized	Stored	Translated
Recommended	Saved	Streamed	Traveled
Reconciled	Scheduled	Streamlined	Treated
Recorded	Scrutinized	Studied	Trialed
Reduced	Secured	Submitted	Troubleshot
Registered	Selected	Suggested	Updated
Reinforced	Served	Supervised	Upgraded
Repaired	Set	Supplied	Uploaded
Replaced	Shared	Supported	Used
Replenished	Simplified	Sustained	Videotaped
Represented	Solved	Taught	Welcomed
Requested	Sought	Tested	Won
Researched	Specified	Toured	Wrote

RÉSUMÉ STEP 11:
Notable Achievements

Notable achievements:
- Promoted from Assistant Manager to Manager
- Instituted COVID-19 protocol based on CDC and federal guidelines
- Conceived, pitched and implemented a 30-day special promotion where guests "check in" via social media platforms (Facebook, Instagram, Twitter) to receive a 5% discount on their dine-in meal, which resulted in 14% higher gross earnings for that period through increased consumption and a greater number of dining guests

Show off your specialness. Beneath the bulleted list of responsibilities and accomplishments, you have the option of including a "Notable achievements" category. These are job-related activities that go **beyond normal day-to-day duties**. Some examples include job promotions you earned, projects that you pitched and implemented, awards you received, new methods you developed, speaking events you led, workshops you organized and committees you've assembled. This is your opportunity to show off all that you've accomplished.

Examples:

Won the Alaska State Health Reporting Award for an article examining the effects of removing fluoride from municipal water in Juneau, Alaska

Promoted from Assistant Manager to Manager within 2 years

Need help remembering your notable achievements at each job? Go to the end of this chapter for a list of **questions to ask yourself** that will jog your memory.

Get specific. If you can, add numbers (such as how many additional products were sold because of your idea), well-known names (such as major trade conferences), links to celebrities and industry powerhouses or other facts that would **stand out** in a hiring manager's mind.

Examples:

Conceived, pitched and launched the company's first social media campaign that resulted in a 12% increase in revenue within the first 3 months

Selected to represent the company on a panel about innovations in the assisted home health care industry at International Health Expo 2019 in Vancouver, Canada

Be discreet. It's helpful to show off special projects you led, problems you fixed and ways you made a company better. However, be careful not to disclose company **secrets, sensitive information or activity related to legal or criminal issues**. One reason is that it may breach a nondisclosure agreement you possibly signed upon accepting your job, putting you at legal risk. Another reason is that being discreet about your previous companies shows potential new employers that you will guard their private information as well.

You can feel free to share notable achievements that involve sensitive information in your résumé. Simply state these situations in **general terms** to protect the company.

Example:

If you discovered fake company checks were being created by an employee:

Spotted irregularities in check processing and worked with senior management to pinpoint and resolve the issue, saving the company more than $13,000

Also important: If asked to give more details about these kinds of sensitive situations in job interviews, politely decline by saying, "Since that company considers this situation confidential, I can't share more information." Interviewers could be asking if you'll elaborate as a way to find out if you **can be trusted with their company's secrets**, too. By keeping a former employer's information private, you'll send the message that you can be trusted by this employer, too.

This section is not mandatory. If you do not have notable accomplishments to include for one or more jobs, don't worry—this section is **optional**.

Questions to Ask Yourself

Need help remembering your notable accomplishments for each job? Interview yourself! Asking yourself the following questions for each position you include in your résumé will help jog your memory so you can add more detail and important information:

- Were you promoted to a new title or role while at the company?

- Were you given any work-related awards or special recognition by the company or by an outside organization for tasks you performed for the company?

- Did you pitch any ideas, projects or changes that were adopted by your supervisor, department or company?

- Did you do anything to help save the company time or money that was not part of your usual job duties, for example, improving a process, adopting a new type of software, finding a different vendor or spotting a problem?

- Were you given a special opportunity? For example, were you asked to represent the company at a conference as a panelist or vendor? Were you invited to lead tours of the factory, campus or building? Were you appointed to a role outside your usual job description, such as COVID-19 safety protocol manager?

- Did you lead a committee or major project that is not in your usual job duties? For example, were you appointed to lead a steering committee or assemble a team to build a company website?

- Did you create anything for the company that is not included in your usual job duties, such as writing a manual or coming up with a new procedure?

- Did you create any media for the company that is outside your usual job description? For example, did you host a podcast, write a blog, write a newsletter, film videos, write video scripts or write, edit or publish a book or an eBook for the company?

- Did a notable person or celebrity interact with any of your work products? For example, did a well-known actor perform in one of your work-related videos? Or did you interview a philanthropist for a work-related podcast?

- Did a notable media outlet take notice of your work? For example, were you interviewed by a major website, magazine or podcast? Or did your work get reviewed in a reputable magazine, newspaper or blog?

- Were you asked to share your work-related expertise or skills outside your workplace, for example, at a conference, in a classroom, at a store, on video, in an article or on a podcast?

- Did you do anything special or outstanding as the leader or a member of a group, team, committee or project you were involved in at work? For example, did you lead a recruitment drive that led to a significant increase in memberships or find a supplier that saved the company money?

- Did you volunteer for a notable activity at work, such as event manager for your company's annual toy drive?

RÉSUMÉ STEP 12:
Education

> **Assistant Restaurant Manager** 2017–2019
> Red Rock Inn, South Bend, Indiana
> - Assisted Restaurant Manager on F.O.H. and B.O.H. operations, including managing payroll, organizing staff schedules and maintaining vendor relationships
> - Coordinated communication between F.O.H. and B.O.H. staff and prepared shift schedules for Manager
> - Kept detailed records of daily, weekly and monthly costs and revenues
> - Arranged for new employees' onboarding (including scheduling training and ordering uniforms)
> - Calculated needs and placed orders for kitchenware and equipment
> - Monitored compliance with safety and hygiene regulations
> - Gathered guest feedback and recommended improvements
>
> **Notable achievements:**
>
> **EDUCATION**
>
> Associate of Arts (A.A.), Culinary Arts and Restaurant Management, 2016
> Pennsylvania Culinary Institute, Pittsburgh, Pennsylvania
>
> **Hostess** 2012–2013
> Waffle Saloon, Gary, Indiana
> - Welcomed guests, engaged in friendly conversation, suggested new menu items and pointed out special promotions
> - Processed payments and made correct change
> - Helped with beverage orders for guests
> - Completed side work, cleaned and assisted other team members as needed
>
> **EDUCATION**
>
> Associate of Arts (A.A.), Culinary Arts and Restaurant Management, 2016
> Pennsylvania Culinary Institute, Pittsburgh, Pennsylvania
>
> **CERTIFICATIONS**
>
> ServSafe Manager Certification, 2017
> Unrestricted Bartending Permit, Indiana Alcohol & Tobacco Commission, 2014
> ServSafe Handler Certification, 2014
> Certified Server, Indiana Alcohol & Tobacco Commission, 2014
>
> **COMPUTER SKILLS**
>
> Google Drive, Microsoft Excel, Microsoft Word, restaurant management software (OpenTable, PeachWorks, Toast), social media (Facebook, Instagram, Twitter)

List diplomas, certifications and trainings. This is the section where you add your **education**. Include trade schools, universities, postgraduate training and education received during service in the armed forces or other institutions. And include other training that resulted in certifications.

Make it simple. Aside from which school to list first, there is no right or wrong way to put the rest of the details in this section. The goal is to simply make it organized by listing each type of school or training **the same way so they're each formatted identically**.

I've chosen the **suggested format below** for you to follow: The first line is the diploma, degree or certification you received, the subject of study and the year you earned it (which is optional if not required by the job). The second line is name of the school and its location. The lines below that are for outstanding achievements in that school or educational institution.

Example:

Bachelor of Arts (B.A.), Visual Art, 2016
Brown University, Providence, Rhode Island
   Notable Achievements:
   Photography Editor, The Brown Daily Herald, 2014, 2015

However, if you prefer a different format—with the school named on the top line for example—that's fine. Just remember to **be consistent** with your formatting if you have more than one item in your Education section. So, if you put the name of your school in the top line for the first item, put the name of your school in the top line for the second item.

Example:

Rochester Institute of Technology, Rochester, New York
Master of Fine Arts (M.F.A.), Photography, 2018

Brown University, Providence, Rhode Island
Bachelor of Arts (B.A.), Visual Art, 2016
   Notable Achievements:
   Photography Editor, The Brown Daily Herald, 2014, 2015

Place the most recent school first. If you have more than one school or educational institution to include, **list the most recent (or current) one you attended first**. Below it, list the one you attended before that. And so on.

Example:

Master of Fine Arts (M.F.A.), Photography, 2018
Rochester Institute of Technology, Rochester, New York

Bachelor of Arts (B.A.), Visual Art, 2016
Brown University, Providence, Rhode Island
   Notable Achievements:
   Photography Editor, The Brown Daily Herald, 2014, 2015

Had multiple types of trainings in one school? If you had more than one type of training or certification from a single institution, list each. The **most recent one** goes first.

Example:

Auxiliary Boiler School, 2013
Boiler Water/Feedwater Chemistry, 2012
US Navy, Little Creek, Virginia

Currently enrolled in school? If you're currently attending a trade school, university or other institution where you'll be receiving a certificate or diploma, go ahead and list it in the Education section of your résumé. Include the certificate or degree you'll be receiving, then **add "Currently Enrolled"**, the name of your school and its location. Add "Expected Graduation" and the anticipated date that you will be graduating.

Examples:

Certified Nursing Assistant (C.N.A), Currently Enrolled
American Red Cross, Oakford, Pennsylvania
Expected Graduation: October 2021

Master of Social Work (M.S.W.), Currently Enrolled
New York University, New York, New York
Expected Graduation: May 2021

What about high school? Whether you list your high school in the Education section of your résumé **depends** on a number of factors:

- **If you do not have a college degree:** If you have not received a college degree and are not pursuing one, **list your high school education**, including the name of your school, type of diploma you received (such as General Diploma or Honors Diploma), the year you earned the degree (which is optional if not required by the employer), the school's location and any notable accomplishments.

    If your high school was **online**, list its name, the type of degree you earned, the year you earned it (which is optional if not required by the employer), its website URL address and any notable accomplishments.

    If you attended **homeschool**, list the name affiliated with the homeschool or describe it as "Independent Homeschool", the type of degree you earned, the year you earned it (which is optional if not required by the employer) and include its location as well as notable achievements from academic-related activities or activities associated with subjects you studied, such as a writing award.

    Examples:

    General Diploma, 2015
    Lincoln High School, South Bend, Indiana

    Honors Diploma, 2017
    Fife High School, Tacoma, Washington
    Notable Achievements:
    Graduated cum laude
    Treasurer of the Debate Club, 2016, 2017

General Diploma, 2015
Mary Parker Academic High School,
MaryParkerAcademicHS.org
   Notable Achievements:
   Vice President of the Engineering Club, 2017

General Education Diploma, 2018
Independent Home School, Denver, Colorado
   Notable Achievements:
   Won 1st prize, Emerging Writer's Contest, 2017

- **If you have a college degree:** If you have graduated from college or are currently enrolled, generally, you do not list your high school education. It's **understood that you attended high school** and received a degree, which is commonly a mandatory requirement for enrollment in a higher education institution.

- **If you have a college degree and your high school experience stands out:** There are certain instances where it can **add value** to your résumé to include your high school education in addition to your college degree, for example, if you attended a prestigious high school, received special honors (such as being named valedictorian) or you had notable achievements that are related to your field. In these cases, beneath your college information, list your high school along with its name, location and any achievements.

Include notable achievements. Underneath the school name, location and degree or certificate you earned, include anything that may be considered **a special accomplishment**. These can include (but are not limited to) the following:

- **School offices** you held, for example, class president or treasurer of a club
- **Awards** you've earned (which include those given by the school as well as those received by an outside organization

for schoolwork, such as a writing award for a short story or athletic award for sports)
- **Grade point average** (G.P.A.) if it was exceptionally high
- **Honors** you received, such as valedictorian or graduating *summa cum laude*
- **School activities** if they are related to your field, such as editor of the school newspaper or treasurer of the Math Club

Example:

Bachelor of Science, Information Technology, 2015
Boston University
   Notable Achievements:
3.8 GPA
Honors Student 2012, 2013, 2014, 2015

Add continued education. Include **postgraduate** courses, **internships, fellowships** and other educational trainings in the Education section if you have it. Place them in order of when you completed these trainings with the most current experiences at the top.

Examples:

John S. Knight Community Impact Fellow, 2020
Stanford University, Stanford, California

One-Year Postgraduate Training Program in Food, Eating and the Body, 2014
Women's Therapy Centre Institute, New York, New York

Add related licenses. If your training led you to obtain a **license**, add it in the Education section.

Examples:

Cosmetology Diploma, Rise Beauty School, 2017
Bayshore, New York
Cosmetology License, New York
Issued May 2017, Expires May 2021

Master of Social Work (M.S.W.), Florida State University
Tallahassee, Florida
Licensed Clinical Social Worker (L.C.S.W.), Florida
Issued May 2018, Expires May 2022

Write out your degree and include its abbreviation. If you received a degree or certification that's also commonly shortened (for example, B.A. for Bachelor of Arts), **include both** the full name of the degree or certification as well as its abbreviation in parentheses next to it. This ensures that résumé-scanning software used by companies to search for keywords finds your qualifications.

A note about graduation years. Do not include the year you graduated if you think it **will negatively impact your chances** of getting invited for an interview due to age discrimination (whether you're younger or older) or other reasons. Let the hiring manager call you in, then win that person over with your skills and enthusiasm for the position.

RÉSUMÉ STEP 13: Computer Skills

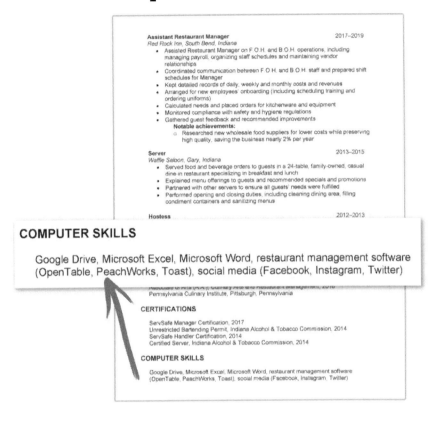

Keep it simple. For most résumés, all you need is **one list** to name the computer software, professional websites and online programs you know how to use that are related to your field or that are required to do the job you want.

However, for **technical positions** in the computing field (such as programmer or website developer), skip this list if you're already including this information in your job descriptions. Alternatively, you can create a longer, more detailed list that's organized by category to fit your industry.

Mention special training. Include **certifications** for any software related to your field. This may be from a short-term independent training you obtained or while enrolled in a university, trade school or other school.

Add social media if required. Include **social media platforms** only if this is related to the job, for example, if you'll be managing social media posts, analyzing social media campaigns or pitching social media projects.

Include the basics. Add **basic general skills** in software programs if you have them, such as "basic Microsoft Excel". This way, if they're needed for simple tasks, employers know you can handle them.

Add extras. Include programs or websites you know how to use that may not be directly related to the available job right now—but could **possibly be used in the future**. For example, the description for the job you're pursuing may not require basic HTML, however, if you think you'll need it if you're promoted from that position to another, then include it.

Organize your list. Put all programs and websites in **alphabetical** order if you're not in a tech-related field. If you are in a tech field, arrange programs and websites in **order of importance** related to the job you're seeking.

Make it proper. Use the **full proper names** of programs and websites (such as "Microsoft Word" instead of "Word") to ensure résumé-scanning software detects them.

> *Example:*
>
> *Basic HTML, ConstantContact, Microsoft Word, social media platforms (Facebook, Instagram, TikTok, Twitter), WordPress*

RÉSUMÉ STEP 14: Optional Sections

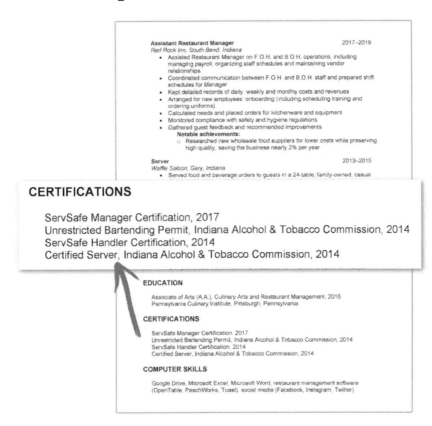

What are "Optional Sections"?

There are a variety of optional sections you can add to your résumé that **show hiring managers even more about you** than what's listed in your standard job descriptions. These optional sections may describe organizations you belong to, volunteer work, a book you wrote, a podcast you host or details about other facets of your life and experience.

The goal with optional sections is to demonstrate **even more reasons** why you're the best candidate for the position. So, you want them to relate in some way to the job opening if possible.

Add and remove optional sections. For your convenience, in the editable, preformatted Word résumé template, there is an optional section for "Certifications". But, you can **change this** to "Memberships", "Volunteer Positions", "Awards", "Publications" or any other section that relates to the position you want.

Need more than one optional section? You can **add more** by simply copying the Certifications section on the template by left-clicking your mouse button and using your mouse to select that section, then pressing Ctrl + c to copy. Put your cursor where you want the new section to be (such as above or below the existing optional section), then press Ctrl + v to paste.

Don't need any optional sections? **Delete** the optional section on the template by simply backspacing over the text or left-clicking your mouse button, using your mouse to select that text, then pressing the Delete key.

Brainstorm optional sections that are right for you.
Below are examples of optional sections you can add to your résumé that highlight your unique experiences, training and accomplishments. But, **don't feel limited by these recommendations**. If there's a category I haven't suggested that relates to your field that you'd like to include on your résumé, then add it.

- **Professional Organizations.** This section is where you list **memberships to professional organizations** you currently have or held in the past that are related to your field. Here's how to list this information on your résumé:

    Organization name, dates you belonged
    Office you hold in the organization (if you hold one), years you were in this office

Examples:

PROFESSIONAL ORGANIZATIONS

Association of Software Professionals, 2017-Present

National Association of Neonatal Nurses, 2011-2017
Treasurer: 2014-2017
Secretary: 2012-2013

- **Volunteer Positions.** If you've been active as a volunteer in **an organization or role that's related to your field**, definitely include it in your résumé.
  And, if your volunteer experience is not related to your field, go ahead and include it, anyway. Not only do most types of volunteer work demonstrate that you have **"soft" skills**—for example, an ability to work as part of a team—your volunteer experience may **highlight other talents** a hiring manager would find helpful for the position, such as social media marketing or event planning know-how. Here's how to list volunteer experience on your résumé:

Office or position and dates you were active
Organization name and location
Responsibilities and accomplishments

Example:

VOLUNTEER POSITIONS

Pet Adoption Marketing Assistant, January 2017-Present
Paws Patrol Rescue, Boston, Massachusetts
- *Take photos and write playful, engaging biographies of cats and dogs available for adoption*

- *Assist Marketing Director with scheduling and planning adoption events inside PetSmart stores 4 times per year, including coordinating with store managers, recruiting volunteers and designing signage*

Note: If you wrote about your volunteer experience as a job in the Professional Experience section of your résumé because you had a gap or you're changing careers, **do not repeat** that information here.

- **Licenses and certifications.** This is where you would name all the **licenses, certifications and special designations** you've been granted that are related to the job you want. List them here even if you have already noted them in other areas of your résumé. Since these are typically important aspects of job requirements, rounding them up in one section ensures the hiring manager sees them. When listing them, each goes on its own separate line.

Examples:

LICENSES AND CERTIFICATIONS

Certified Public Accountant (C.P.A.) licensed by the Florida Board of Accountancy

New York City High Pressure Boiler Operating Engineer License

Certified in Cardiopulmonary Resuscitation (C.P.R.) from Red Cross

Honors and awards. This is where you would list honors, awards or other **accolades you've earned**, which can include fellowships, talks and special recognitions. Here's how to list this information on your résumé:

Honor, title (if applicable), location, date

Examples:

HONORS AND AWARDS

Fellowship, National Endowment for the Arts, Washington, D.C., 2012

TEDx Featured Speaker, "Righting the Wrongs of the Sales Industry," Orlando, Florida, June 1, 2019

- **Military service.** If you served in the military, you may want to include it in your résumé. In some cases, candidates with an Armed Forces background are given **priority in the application process**. Your military experience may also make you more qualified for the job you're seeking because of **skills you obtained during your service**. Here's how to list this information on your résumé:

Your branch of the Armed Forces, rank, last position held, years you served
Responsibilities and accomplishments
Status of discharge

Example:

MILITARY SERVICE

United States Navy, Sergeant, Boiler Technician 3rd Class 1984-1988
- *Responsible for the operation and maintenance of the ship's auxiliary boilers and evaporators, main diesel engines, generators, propulsion systems, medium pressure air compressors, low pressure air*

>   compressors, fire systems, safety training
>   and boiler water/feedwater chemistry
> - Honorably discharged

- **Publications.** This is a list of books, magazine articles, blog posts, studies and other published written works that **you've personally authored or co-authored**. Here's how to list this information on your résumé:

Title, place of publication or publisher, date of publication
Optional: A brief description of the published work

> *Examples:*
>
> **PUBLICATIONS**
>
> *The Growing Problem in Garden Centers, GardenLove.com, May 23, 2020*
> - An online article examining the effects of the popularity of non-native invasive species of decorative plants sold at garden centers on native habitats
>
> *A Nurse's Handbook, Healthwise Publishing, 2018*
> - A 112-page paperback guide to help new nurses adjust to the demands of the field while avoiding burnout

- **Podcasts.** This is a list of podcasts **you've hosted or participated in** that relate to the job you're seeking. Here's how to list this information on your résumé:

Podcast name, podcast episode title (if being interviewed), date
Details about the podcast

Examples:

PODCASTS

Taking a Bite Out of Restaurants Podcast, 2017-Present
- Host of a weekly podcast that explores news and trends in the restaurant industry

Eatery Café Podcast, "The New Dine-In Experience," May 23, 2020
- Interviewed by host Meagan Brown about dine-in changes in independently-owned restaurants during the COVID-19 pandemic

- **Blogs.** This is a list of blogs that you **own, edit, curate or write for** that are related to the job you want. For example, if you're in the hospitality industry, you might review restaurants. If you're a website developer, you may report on the latest security apps you use to keep websites secure. Here's how to list this information on your résumé:

Blog name, blog website address, article title (if being interviewed), date
Details about the blog

Examples:

BLOGS

Teacher's Teaching (TeachersTeaching.com), 2018-Present
- Write blog that shares daily helpful tips for elementary, middle-school, junior high school and high school teachers

Drawing Your Way to Better Math Skills,
Teacher's Teaching blog
(TeachersTeaching.com), May 23, 2018
- *Guest blogger for a popular blog sharing tips for teachers by teachers*

RÉSUMÉ STEP 15:
Edit Your Résumé

The unfortunate truth is that spelling and grammar mistakes on your résumé can hurt your chances of being called in for an interview. For most industries, one or two errors won't be a deal-breaker. So, **don't stress over missing a typo**. Most interviewers let a couple of inadvertent goofs slide. Typically, only folks applying for writing and editing positions will require a perfect résumé to qualify for an interview.

But, even if you're not a writer or editor, it's still a good idea to try to keep mistakes to a minimum since you'll look more **professional and detail-oriented**. Following are tactics professional writers and editors use to catch mistakes...

Ask Microsoft Word to spot errors. Run Microsoft Word's automatic **spell check and grammar check**. You'll find these under "Editor" on the far upper right of your Word screen. These programs will point out misspelled words, grammar issues and other problems you may have.

Important: While this program is helpful, don't blindly agree to *all* the changes it recommends. **Sometimes, this program is wrong**, for example, when you write the name of a software program or business. While hiring managers will typically overlook a missing "and" or misspelled "achieved", they won't be so forgiving if you misspell the name of a computer program needed to do the job. So, use the Internet or another resource to double-check these kinds of changes before you agree to them.

Talk it out. Read every line of your résumé slowly **out loud**. This is a tried-and-true trick that professional writers use to make sure they didn't accidentally skip a word, include a typo or forget to finish a sentence. It also helps you hear how a phrase sounds to ensure it's written in the best way.

Start at the bottom. Now read your résumé **out loud backwards**! Meaning, read the last line first, then the next to last line, then the line before that. This is another trick professional writers rely on to make sure they didn't accidentally skip over a missing word or typo. That's because it forces you to pay closer attention to each word in each line.

Get help from pals. Ask, beg, plead, even bribe friends and family members to read your résumé. **More eyes** on your résumé means more chances of catching a mistake. They may also have valuable feedback that helps you rephrase lines a better way or they may remind you of responsibilities and accomplishments that you forgot.

Cover Letter DIY Guide

Everything you need to create your own professional-quality cover letter

You get...
✓ Easy step-by-step instructions
✓ Editable, preformatted Word templates
✓ Insider tips and tricks from a pro

Cover Letter-Writing Introduction

Stand out from the crowd...and be remembered

Heard that cover letters are old-fashioned or unnecessary? Not true! In a recent survey, **58% of senior managers** said they view cover letters as a "very valuable" part of the hiring process.[1] No wonder: Including a cover letter with your job application gives you the opportunity to…

- ✓ Display your **passion** for your industry
- ✓ Show your **enthusiasm** for the business where you want to work
- ✓ **Explain** work gaps, short-term positions or why you're changing jobs or careers
- ✓ Share important or interesting **details about yourself** not included in your résumé
- ✓ Let your **personality** shine through

This **Cover Letter-Writing DIY Guide** will help you meet all these goals. It quickly and easily guides you through every step of crafting the kind of cover letter that makes you stand out from the crowd and be remembered long after the hiring manager finishes reading.

LET'S GET STARTED:

1. Read the General Cover Letter-Writing Tips.

2. Move on to the easy
Step-by-Step Cover Letter-Writing Instructions.

---

[1] RH-US.mediaroom.com/2020-01-08-Survey-Reveals-Job-Search-Trends-For-2020

General Cover Letter-Writing Tips

Before you start writing your cover letter, please review these general cover letter-writing tips. They'll help make the whole process easier for you:

✓ **Send a cover letter almost <u>every time</u>**

Nearly 6 in 10 senior managers say they want job applicants to submit a cover letter with their résumé. This means a majority of folks in charge of hiring expect to see a cover letter—and they'll be basing their decision on who to invite to a job interview in part on whether the cover letter is included in their application.

What this means for you: By sending a cover letter every time you respond to a job ad, you automatically boost your chances of getting invited to be interviewed.

❓ *But, what if the job ad doesn't specifically ask for a cover letter?*

Send yours, anyway.

❓ *But, what if everyone else you know isn't submitting cover letters?*

Send yours, anyway.

❓ *But, what if a friend who's a hiring manager told you she doesn't bother reading cover letters at her job?*

Send yours, anyway.

The only times you definitely do *not* submit a cover letter are when applying for positions where one is clearly not appropriate, for example, when filling out an in-person job application at a retail store.

Also skip it if the job ad specifically states that cover letters will not be read.

All other times, send your cover letter. It shows you're willing to take that extra step to get the interview, which demonstrates passion and enthusiasm—traits employers seek.

 Backspace, then replace the text on the cover letter template

When adding your own text to the editable, preformatted Word cover letter template, use the backspace button to remove each line of sample text in each section as you go through the step-by-step instructions. Backspacing will preserve the formatting (such as font, type size, bullets, indents, etc.) so the new text you add looks like the old text you're replacing.

If you try to select a block of text, then press delete, you may lose the formatting.

✓ **Undo if you need a do-over**

Made a mistake when changing the editable, preformatted Word cover letter template? Not a problem. You can use the "undo" arrow (on the top left of your Word screen) or press Ctrl + z to make a correction. If you need to start over from scratch, simply download the editable, preformatted Word résumé template again. There is no limit to how many times you can download it.

✓ **Stick to one page when possible**

Cover letters are best when they're brief and to the point. Sticking to one page—with about four to five paragraphs—is optimal.

However, there will be times when a two-page cover letter is needed and even better, for example, if you want to describe your managerial style and include quick anecdotes. Or the job ad may request additional information be included in your cover letter, which may take up more space.

✓ **Change the cover letter with <u>every</u> job application**

Just like you tailor your résumé for every job application, you'll want to customize your cover letter, too. That's because you may want to stress different skills or experience based on what the employer is looking for. Plus, you'll want to explain why you're applying for that particular company—a must-have for every successful cover letter.

✓ **Do <u>not</u> aim for perfection**

Many job seekers can get overwhelmed when writing a cover letter because they aren't comfortable writing, in general. It's okay if you aren't comfortable either. Just try to remember that you do not have to write the "perfect" cover letter. Hiring managers aren't looking for the best-written cover letter…unless you're actually applying for a writing, editing or marketing position. For most other positions, what most employers want from your cover letter is simply to get the *overall gist* of…

- The **enthusiasm** you have for the job, your field and their company
- Additional information about your **skills or experience**
- Anything else that tells them you're the **better candidate**

So, try not to stress about using the best phrases or coming up with the best lines. Simply sending in any cover letter already raises your chances of beating out other applicants since most hiring managers expect to see one and many job applicants don't bother to submit it at all.

Step-by-Step Cover Letter-Writing Instructions

Above is what your cover letter will end up looking like by the time you're finished.

All you have to do is follow the simple **Step-by-Step Cover Letter-Writing Instructions** that follow. They'll show you how to create a cover letter that gets hiring managers reading past the first paragraph and helps them remember you long after they're done.

Get started:

Download the editable, preformatted Microsoft Word résumé template:

GabrielleLichterman.com/DIYTemplates

COVER LETTER STEP 1:
Header

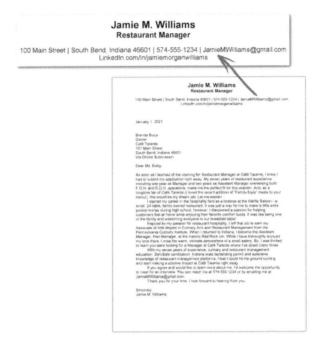

Make it match. The name, professional title, contact information and LinkedIn URL address on your cover letter should match what's on your résumé—such as the same placement on the page and font size. You want to make the cover letter and résumé look like they **belong together as if they're a set**. The editable Word template has already formatted the headers so they're identical so you don't have to worry about this. But, keep this tip in mind for the future in case you make any changes.

Check out the résumé instructions. If you haven't written your résumé yet, check out the résumé-writing section for details on **how to write** each part of your header so you can apply it to your cover letter.

COVER LETTER STEP 2: Date

Include the date. Type the date you're submitting your cover letter for the job on the **upper left** two to four lines below your contact information and LinkedIn URL address. Write the date fully without using abbreviations, spelling out the month.

Example:

January 1, 2021

If the date is written **differently** in your region, country or career field, feel free to change it to adapt to that style, for example "1 January, 2021".

COVER LETTER STEP 3:
Company Address

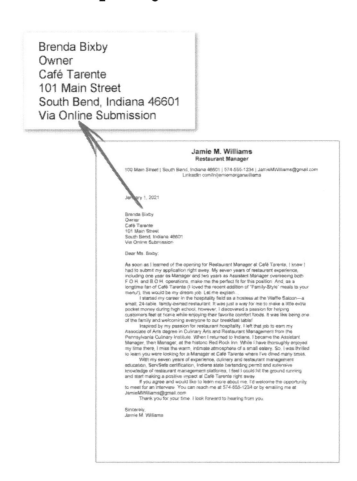

Add the recipient's information. Two lines **below the date**, type the name of the person you're submitting your application to and their title. Below that, type the company's name and mailing address. Below that, include an email address if you are submitting your application via email.

Example:

Jean Gates
Manager
Tier Accounting Services, LLP
202 Raybaud Street
Huntington Woods, Michigan 48070
JeanGates@TierAccountingSvc.biz

No name available? If you do not have **the name of the person** who is receiving the submission:

- **Surf the web.** Look on the company's website or LinkedIn profile to see if you can find the manager for the department that has the opening. It's always better to put a name on your cover letter when possible.

- **Be general.** If you can't find a name, address your cover letter to "Human Resources".

    Example:

    Human Resources
    Tier Accounting Services, LLP
    202 Raybaud Street
    Huntington Woods, Michigan 48070

No mailing address? If you do not have the **company's snail mail address**, try to find it on their website or by doing an online search. If you can't find one, simply skip it and only include the email address where you're submitting the application.

Example:

Human Resources
Tier Accounting Services, LLP
Recruiting@TierAccountingSvc.biz

Applying online? If you're using a company's online recruiting software to **upload** your résumé and cover letter and don't have an email address to add to your submission, then simply type, "Online Submission".

Examples:

Human Resources
Tier Accounting Services, LLP
202 Raybaud Street
Huntington Woods, Michigan 48070
Online Submission

Human Resources
Tier Accounting Services, LLP
Online Submission

COVER LETTER STEP 4:
Greeting

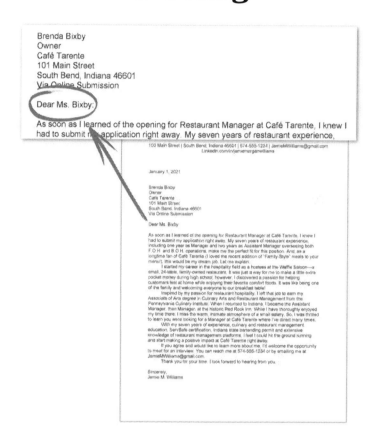

State their name. When greeting the person reading your cover letter, use the **name** mentioned in the job ad.

If there isn't a name mentioned in the ad, **search** the company's website or look up the company on LinkedIn to find the manager of the department that has the job opening or a name of a human resources director. They can often be found there.

It's always better to include a name when you can. Even if the person you found is not the one who's reviewing applications, taking that one extra step makes you look **familiar with the company** and eager to be interviewed than someone who used a generic greeting without a name.

Make it professional. Use a **formal greeting** (such as Mr. or Ms.) if you are certain of the recipient's gender. If you are uncertain of their gender, some people state their preferred pronouns in their company's online biography or their social media account bio. So, look there.

No name? If you cannot find a name, simply type, **"Dear Sir or Madam"**.

Format it right. Use a **colon (:)**, which is the traditional punctuation for a greeting in a professional letter. (Commas are typically for informal greetings between friends and close peers, not business professionals.)

Examples:

Dear Ms. Miles:

Dear Mr. Blum:

Dear Sir or Madam:

COVER LETTER STEP 5: Introductory Paragraph

Make it memorable. Your cover letter shouldn't be a dull rehash of what's already in your résumé. Instead, it's an opportunity to show employers your passion for their company and enthusiasm for your field and to make a **positive first impression** that sticks with them long after they finish reading. And all this starts with your first paragraph.

Chances are, more than 90% of the cover letters a hiring manager receives will start this **boring old way**: *"I'm writing to submit my résumé for such-and-such position."*

By opening your cover letter with something—anything!—different, you'll already **stand out** from the other applicants.

So, get creative, be bold and dare to show just how much you want this particular job. This will shake the hiring manager out of a haze of boredom and **capture their attention**. Even in industries that require a fairly dry, formal approach (such as legal and medical fields), a little tweak can make a big difference.

Check out the rest of the following tips for what makes a great first paragraph for a cover letter. Then, **review the examples** at the end of this chapter to see how all the tips come together so you can get inspired to write your own stand-out opening lines that stick in the hiring manager's mind.

Mention the job opening. Include the **title of the job** that's available. Hiring managers often have many positions open, so this ensures they're considering you for the job you want.

Include the company's name. State the **name** of the business where you're applying. This sends the message that you have a special interest in the company, which virtually all hiring managers want to see.

Did you find the job a special way? State **how you found out** about the job opening if it can help boost your chances of getting a call for an interview.

For example, were you **referred by someone** who currently works there or worked there in the past? If so, include their name as well as their job title if you know it. You do not have to say how you know each other. (You can save that for the job interview.)

Or did you find the opening on a **company's job board**, which is typically on their own website? If so, state it. Employers love when you seek out their company specifically. It indicates you're probably already a good fit and will stick around awhile. (*Tip:* If you found a job opening on Indeed.com or another employment website, search the company's own job board to see if they posted the same position. Then in your cover letter, say you found it there.)

Why are you applying? Briefly explain **why you want this job**: Is it because you were excited by the position? A fan of the company? You're changing jobs? Switching careers? You share the same goals? Touch on the reason (don't go into lots of detail just yet) and try to show enthusiasm.

Assure employers you're a great match. Mention that your **experience matches this job** perfectly. Don't go into too much detail in this paragraph, but convince the reader that you've looked over their list of qualifications and judged that your experience and skills match it. This encourages them to read further.

For example, cite two of the **top qualifications** the ad is looking for, such as, *"I have the 5 years of graphic design experience and mastery of Adobe Photoshop you're looking for."*

Or you can mention **well-known companies** where you've worked, which is a shortcut for explaining that your experience matches the job. Plus, it raises your status. For example, *"After working 3 years at Proctor & Gamble, I'm eager to join the non-profit world and use my graphic design expertise to help others."*

Add *this* secret success tip every single time. Tack on the phrase **"Let me explain…"** to the end of the first paragraph in your cover letter. This is nifty little trick makes the paragraph more interesting while guaranteeing the hiring manager will read on.

Examples:

TO SHOW YOUR ENTHUSIASM:
As soon as I learned of the opening for Social Media Coordinator for Ruby Shoes Boutique, I knew I had to submit my application. My 3 years as a Social Media professional plus B.A. in fashion marketing make me the perfect fit for this position. And, as a longtime fan of Ruby Shoes apparel and footwear (your recent Spring line's "Back to Nature" theme was your best yet!), this would

be my dream job. Let me explain...

TO GO BOLD:
Let me start by saying that I wouldn't be applying to become Bigshot Magazine's next Senior Graphic Designer if I wasn't fully confident that I was the right person for this position. I realize this is a bold statement to make right out of the gate, but I happen to have the unique blend of experience and skills you're seeking. Let me explain...

IF YOU'RE SWITCHING JOBS OR CAREERS:
When I learned that Syracuse University was seeking an Accounts Payable Supervisor from the university's job board, I knew immediately I had to apply. That's because, even though I enjoy my current position as an Accounts Payable Supervisor for Morgan Stanley, I'm certain that I can make a more impactful positive contribution by sharing my well-honed financial skills in a higher education setting. Let me explain...

IF YOU HAVE A REFERRAL FROM SOMEONE:
As soon as Mary Burns, a wait staff team member at Kafka House Café, told me about the open Restaurant Manager position, I knew I had to submit my résumé. That's because I have the 5 years of front-of-house experience and restaurant metrics skills you're seeking. Plus, this is exact type of Restaurant Manager position I've been hoping to find. Let me explain...

IF YOU'RE IN A HIGHLY FORMAL FIELD (SUCH AS MEDICAL OR LEGAL):
I am eager to submit my application for the position of Legal Assistant/Paralegal at Dawn, Finch and Associates, LLC. Not only do I have the exact qualifications you are seeking, this is the position I have been hoping to find. Let me explain...

COVER LETTER STEP 6:
Body of Your Letter

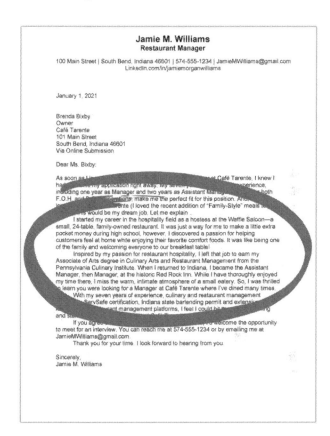

Make it a story. The greatest writers know one important secret: **Personal stories are more memorable than plain facts**.

That's because they pull you in and make you want to **learn more**. They also help the reader connect with you, so you stay on their mind longer.

For a cover letter, there are other benefits of sharing personal details: They can help you **fill in missing pieces**, such as explaining work gaps or career changes, by adding context.

Therefore, when writing the rest of your cover letter, try to write it in a way that **tells a story about you** while sharing the reasons you're the best candidate for the job.

Also helpful: When you can, try to add an **interesting anecdote or quirky detail**, such as being paid in chocolate fudge for your first job. This adds color to your cover letter, making you stand out from the other candidates.

If you're not comfortable getting personal or you're in a highly formal field, then simply weave together facts about your experience in a **conversational** way.

Following are a few suggested **story styles and examples** to inspire you to craft your own memorable story for your cover letter:

- **The "enthusiastic" story.** Write about **why you love** this particular job opening, your field and/or the company to which you're applying. Many businesses want to ensure you not only have the right skills, but possess a passion for the industry (so you'll want to stick around) and are a good fit for the company's culture (so they'll want you to stick around). Include interesting tidbits about yourself, if possible, to make your letter even more memorable.

    Unfamiliar with the company? **Research** it online to find out more about their culture: Are they forward-thinking and adopt new technologies? Are they focused on helping others? Do they pride themselves on following a traditional way of doing things that's been passed down from former generations? Touch on how their mission aligns with your own goals.

    If you can't find out more about their culture, then touch on their company's **goals in general**: Is it a school? Hospital? Start-up company? Mention how their type of business or institution is what you hope to contribute your skills, expertise and talents to.

    Examples:

    It's been a longtime passion of mine to be a Content Creator. It started when I was 17 and designed my first custom WordPress blog for an orthotic shoe store in my hometown of Elmira, New York. By the time I graduated college, I'd created 18 more WordPress sites for other retail and restaurant clients as an independent contractor. But, what I'd really love most is to join the Content Creation team at Agape Films. I've been a fan of the groundbreaking documentaries that Agape has been producing since its inception in 2014. And I'm inspired by the supportive team-building ethic Agape has become famous for. It would be a privilege to help deliver Agape's important message of education and discovery to a larger audience through artfully-crafted website copy, social media campaigns, blog posts, photos, videos and virtual events.

Many people grow up dreaming of being a teacher. I didn't. I wanted to be a lawyer. I pictured all the cases I'd litigate. The motions I would file. Even the many times I'd announce, "I object!" in the courtroom. Then, Ms. Clarence, my sophomore year Spanish teacher at Ohio State University, came into my life. Her unending patience and support as I struggled to master the second language was an inspiration. It made me realize my true passion wasn't litigation in a courtroom—it was helping others in a classroom. At the end of that semester, I switched majors to Education and never looked back. I'm applying to Riverside Academy as your next 12th-grade History Teacher because I know your school has the same passion for helping students learn that I do. And I'd welcome the opportunity to help you achieve that educational goal.

- **The "special skills" story.** Do you have a skill, talent, certification, degree or experience that makes you **stand out**? For example, are you a retired military member with unique training? Did you work for a well-known person in your field, such as Bill Gates? Did you have a double major in college (such as engineering and a second language), so you have two sets of skills that can be used in the position you want?

    If you do, don't rely on the hiring manager to spot it among the many other facts in your résumé. **Describe what makes you special** in your cover letter to ensure it won't be missed.

    Examples:

    During my time as a Sergeant in the Marines, I was specially trained to find and detect fake social media accounts that were spreading false information or that served as a hub for organizing illegal activities.

    I had the privilege of working alongside noted playwright Shelly Barts (of "Home and Country") and famed director Maggie Brown (best known for "Repeal, Repeal"), who helped me hone my own directing skills.

- **The "gaps explanation" story.** If you have a **gap in employment** that you think may negatively impact your chances of getting called in for an interview, briefly explain why. The people reading your résumé often understand these kinds of circumstances because either they've been in a similar one or know someone who has.

    Examples:

    I took a year off to be the primary caregiver for my partner during intensive cancer treatment.

But, with that chapter of my life now closed, I'm eager to return to work and make a positive contribution in a tax accounting office.

I left my position of Assistant Store Manager of Home Depot to focus 2 years on completing my Bachelor of Business Administration degree in Business Management from Miami University. Once I graduated, I returned to Home Depot as a Store Manager, a job that I held for 2 years.

- **The "exit explanation" story.** If you are **leaving a job** you currently have, briefly explain why. Giving context for an exit reassures hiring managers that you don't jump around. They want to know if you join their team, they can rely on you to stick around awhile.

    Examples:

    As my attached résumé attests, I'm a certified paralegal with 10 years of experience as a judicial secretary in the civil courts. While I have thoroughly enjoyed my tenure in the court system, the judge I have been assisting has decided to retire in July. Therefore, it's time for me to move on and find a new opportunity that allows me to use my extensive background in legal assistance, finely-honed research skills and ability to juggle multiple tasks in a fast-paced setting. The position of Paralegal/Judicial Assistant at Fairfax Legal Group is the exact role I've been hoping to find.

    While I enjoy my current position as a Case Manager at Rising Phoenix Care, my move to Arizona was a temporary one to care for an ailing parent. With that chapter of my life now closed,

> *I'm ready to permanently move back home to Ohio and take on a new position where I can apply the same high level of conscientiousness, teamwork and dedication I've been honing for the past 2 years. The Case Manager position you have open at Focus Care of Toledo is the exact role I've been hoping to find.*

- **The "career change" story.** If you are **changing fields**, briefly explain why. Hiring managers understand that many people learn new skills and enter new careers later in life. When you can, try to show how the skills or experience from your former field come in handy for the new one.

    Examples:

    > While I have thoroughly enjoyed being a restaurant manager, drastic shifts in the economy that have directly impacted the restaurant industry mean it's the right time for me to move on to another field I'm passionate about: health care. Fortunately, it's a transition I'm well-prepared to make. My 6 years in hospitality have helped me hone my customer care skills—such as effective communication, diplomacy and a genuine desire to help others—which are the same skills needed to support patients.

    > My career as a tax accountant has been fulfilling, however, I've realized the time is right for me to pursue another longtime passion: teaching history in a high school setting. While at first these may seem like very different goals requiring vastly different skill sets, truth is, my 15 years as a tax accountant helped me hone the very skills that will make me a capable, impactful teacher at Middlesex High School: patience, attention to

detail and the ability to communicate complex concepts and numerous facts in a way that makes them easily understood and remembered.

- **The "professional strength" story.** If you can fit it in, briefly describe an anecdote that **demonstrates one of your strongest skills or talents** that's needed for the job you want, such as your managerial style. Personal stories that demonstrate your professional abilities are remembered far longer than dry facts.

    Examples:

    While Manager of the Accounts Payable department at PDC Energy Corp., I prided myself on ensuring that all staff members were motivated to take advantage of coaching and mentoring opportunities that would help them grow and sharpen their skills. I recall one time a member of my team turned down the company's offer to pay for her certification in PeopleSoft software. When I inquired why, it turned out she didn't feel she would pass since she didn't see herself as "computer savvy". To help her overcome this lack of confidence, I gave her an introductory lesson so she could get familiar with the software and see for herself that she was, indeed, as capable as I saw her. This staffer went on to take the PeopleSoft certification class and pass with flying colors. After that, she was always the first of my team to sign up for new software classes.

    I'm known as the go-to person for out-of-the-box ideas when you need them. One example: When the owner of West Haven Health Services asked my supervisors to come up with an innovative way to promote their new diabetes testing initiative, their first step was to ask me. Within an hour, I came up with 3 creative concepts—one of which was approved and implemented, leading to a 24% increase in patient testing.

- **The "traditional" story.** If you're more comfortable staying firmly within the **conventional cover letter** box, this traditional style of cover letters is for you. With this letter, you'll go into a little more detail (not a lot) about the skills and experience that make you the right candidate for the position. Make it memorable by adding a small personal detail, such as mentioning your favorite part of your job (such as working with clients) or a brief anecdote about your experience (for example, that you started out in an entry-level position and worked your way up to a managerial or executive role).

    Examples:

    For 2 years, I was the Associate Director of Graphic Design for the Hapstein Glass Museum in Boulder, Colorado. During my time there, I designed a wide array of materials supporting communications, marketing and development both in print and online. These included brochures, fundraising campaigns, newsletters and website copy. My favorite part of the job was finding unique ways to showcase forthcoming exhibits with graphics that matched the artists' voices while also preserving the museum's distinct style.

    I've been in the hospitality field for 8 years—starting as Back Office Assistant for the Luxe Resort in San Diego and working my way up to Spa Manager and later Director of Hotel Sales at D'Or Hotel in Reno, Nevada. My wide spectrum

> of experience in the industry gives me the ability to keenly understand and manage the needs of hotel staff, guests and owners. Coupled with my Certificate in Hotel Management from Harper College, I'm uniquely qualified to take on the role of Manager for the Grand Marino Resort Hotel.

Tie it up with a summary. This is an **optional** part of your cover letter. It helps tie your story to the closing (see Cover Letter Step 7). To do it, sum up the most important facets of your work history, education and/or training, then state how this would benefit the company. After that in the following paragraph (your closing), add "If you agree and would like to learn more about me...", then the rest of your closing.

Examples:

> With my 7 years of experience, culinary and restaurant management education, ServSafe certification, Indiana state bartending permit and extensive knowledge of restaurant management platforms, I feel I could hit the ground running and start making a positive impact at Café Tarente right away.
> If you agree and would like to learn more about me, I'd welcome the opportunity to meet for an interview.

> With my 3 years in retail sales, 1 year as Assistant Manager at a Spectrum Retail Store and proven ability to exceed sales goals and customer care metrics, I'm certain I could help TriState Cable Networks ensure that its current customers are fully satisfied while also fostering loyal relationships with new customers.
> If you agree and would like to learn more about me, I'd welcome the opportunity to meet for an interview.

Do not try to make it perfect. Many job seekers can feel overwhelmed when writing a cover letter, especially if you don't feel that you're a strong writer. But, truth is, unless you're in a field where you're being judged on your writing skills (such as an editor or copy writer), you're improving your chances of being invited for a job interview simply by submitting **virtually *any* cover letter**. That's because most applicants do not submit cover letters despite the majority of hiring managers wanting to receive one.

So, don't worry about getting your words, phrases or even grammar exactly right (if you're not in a writing field, of course). Instead, focus on **simply sharing a story** that explains why you're the best person for the job.

PRO TIP

Type only one space after the period at the end of sentences. Some people still type two spaces (which used to be taught in typing classes), however, this is considered outdated and can make you appear as if you don't keep up with the times, including changes in your field.

COVER LETTER STEP 7: Closing

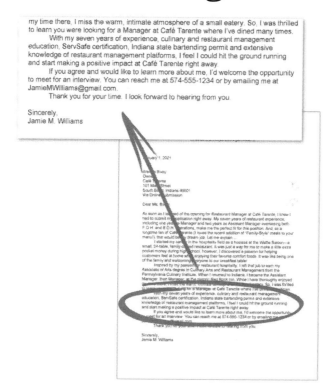

Ask for an interview. The closing is the end of your letter—the final one to three short paragraphs. One key must-have in this section is letting the hiring manager know **you're available to schedule an interview**.

Add your contact information. Include a **phone number and email address** where you can be contacted. Even though this is in your header, it's always a good idea to repeat it at the end of your letter.

Thank the reader. Include a **thank you** to the hiring manager for their time and tell that person you look forward to hearing back.

Keep it short. In most cases, a **simple and straightforward** closing is best. But, feel free to briefly remind the reader what makes you stand out, for example, your experience or special skills.

If you are in a highly creative field where ingenuity and originality are going to help you land the job, you may want to try a more creative closing.

For all other career fields, follow the simple examples below.

Examples:

>*If you'd like to learn more about me by arranging for an interview, please call me at (555) 555-5555 or email me at name@gmail.com.*
>
>*Thank you for your time. I look forward to hearing from you.*

>*If you'd like to learn more about me and the kind of creativity and social media know-how I can bring to Four Score, I'd welcome the opportunity to schedule an interview. You can reach me at (555) 555-5555 or name@gmail.com.*
>
>*Thank you for your time. I look forward to hearing from you.*

>*With my 7 years in restaurant management and professional culinary training, I feel I could hit the ground running and start making a positive impact at Lakewood Café right away.*
>
>*If you agree and would like to learn more about me, I'd welcome the opportunity to schedule an interview. You can reach me at (555) 555-5555 or name@gmail.com.*
>
>*Thank you for your time. I look forward to hearing from you.*

COVER LETTER STEP 8:
Signature

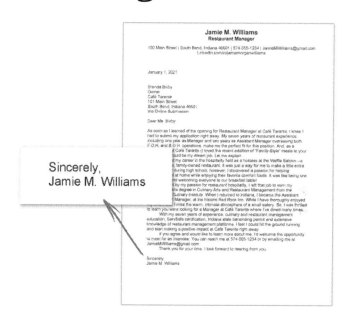

Keep it professional. To end your cover letter, type "Sincerely". It's the traditional way to end a professional letter.

However, if the traditional way to sign off is **different in your region**, use that word or phrase instead.

How to sign it electronically. If you're submitting your cover letter **via email or uploading to a website** (which is going to be the case most times), type your full name underneath "Sincerely".

Example:

Sincerely,
Parker G. Neelam

Sign the paper version. If you are submitting a **hard copy** of your cover letter in the mail or in person, type "Sincerely", then press enter four times and type your full name. Use a pen to write your full signature (first and last name) in the blank space between "Sincerely" and your typed name. If there isn't enough space on your page for four lines in-between, fit as many as you can to be able to squeeze in your signature.

Example:

Sincerely,

Parker G. Neelam

COVER LETTER STEP 9:
Edit Your Cover Letter

The unfortunate truth is that spelling and grammar mistakes on your cover letter can hurt your chances of being called in for an interview. For most industries, one or two errors won't be a deal-breaker. So, **don't stress over missing a typo**. Most interviewers let a couple of inadvertent goofs slide. Typically, only folks applying for writing and editing positions will require a perfect cover letter to qualify for an interview.

But, even if you're not a writer or editor, it's still a good idea to try to keep mistakes to a minimum since you'll look more **professional and detail-oriented**. Following are tactics professional writers and editors use to catch mistakes…

Ask Microsoft Word to spot errors. Run Microsoft Word's automatic **spell check and grammar check**. You'll find these under "Editor" on the far upper right of your Word screen. These programs will point out misspelled words, grammar issues and other problems you may have.

Important: While this program is helpful, don't blindly agree to *all* the changes it recommends. **Sometimes, this program is wrong**, for example, when you write the name of a software program or business. While hiring managers will typically overlook a missing "and" or misspelled "achieved", they won't be so forgiving if you misspell the name of a computer program needed to do the job. So, use the Internet or another resource to double-check these kinds of changes before you agree to them.

Talk it out. Read every line of your cover letter slowly **out loud**. This is a tried-and-true trick that professional writers use to make sure they didn't accidentally skip a word, include a typo or forget to finish a sentence. It also helps you hear how a phrase sounds to ensure it's written the best way.

Start at the bottom. Now read your résumé **out loud backwards**! Meaning, read the last line first, then the next to last line, then the line before that. This is another trick professional writers rely on to make sure they didn't accidentally skip over a missing word or typo. That's because it forces you to pay closer attention to each word in each line.

Get help from pals. Ask, beg, plead, even bribe friends and family members to read your cover letter. **More eyes** on your cover letter means more chances of catching a mistake. They may also have valuable feedback that helps you rephrase lines a better way or they may remind you of responsibilities and accomplishments you forgot.

Résumé Examples

To view PDF versions of these résumé examples, visit GabrielleLichterman.com/DIYTemplates

Jamie M. Williams
Restaurant Manager

100 Main Street | South Bend, Indiana 46601 | 574-555-1234 | JamieMWilliams@gmail.com
LinkedIn.com/in/jamiemorganwilliams

HIGHLIGHTS

- 7 years of restaurant experience, including 1 year as Manager and 2 years as Assistant Manager in casual, dine-in restaurants
- Associate of Arts (A.A.) degree in Culinary Arts and Restaurant Management from Pennsylvania Culinary Institute
- Certified ServSafe Manager and Certified Server from the Indiana Alcohol & Tobacco Commission
- Unrestricted Bartending Permit from the Indiana Alcohol & Tobacco Commission
- Proficient in OpenTable, PeachWorks and Toast restaurant management platforms
- Conceived, pitched and implemented a social media promotional campaign for the Red Rock Inn, resulting in 14% higher gross earnings over 30 days

RESTAURANT EXPERIENCE

Restaurant Manager   2019-Current
Red Rock Inn, South Bend, Indiana
- Manage high-volume, casual, dine-in restaurant with more than $2 million in annual revenue
- Oversee front of house (F.O.H.) and back of house (B.O.H.) operations, including managing payroll, organizing staff schedules and maintaining vendor relationships
- Supervise 24 team members, including assistant manager, waitstaff and bartenders
- Maintain employee ServSafe and Basset certificates and conduct daily inspection of restaurant and equipment to ensure compliance with health, safety, food handling and hygiene standards
- Ensure compliance with alcoholic beverage regulations
- Assist with marketing, group sales and special promotions
- Train team members on proper customer service protocols, new products and software
- Track and control food and beverage costs
- Respond to guest concerns and complaints to quickly and amicably resolve issues in-person and online
  Notable achievements:
    - Promoted from Assistant Manager to Manager
    - Instituted COVID-19 protocol based on CDC guidelines
    - Conceived, pitched and implemented a 30-day special promotion where guests check in via social media platforms (Facebook, Instagram, Twitter) to receive a 5% discount on their dine-in meal, which resulted in 14% higher gross earnings for that period through increased consumption and a greater number of dining guests

Assistant Restaurant Manager   2017–2019
Red Rock Inn, South Bend, Indiana
- Assisted Restaurant Manager on F.O.H. and B.O.H. operations, including managing payroll, organizing staff schedules and maintaining vendor relationships
- Coordinated communication between F.O.H. and B.O.H. staff and prepared shift schedules for Manager
- Kept detailed records of daily, weekly and monthly costs and revenues
- Arranged for new employees' onboarding, including scheduling training and ordering uniforms
- Calculated needs and placed orders for kitchenware and equipment
- Monitored compliance with safety and hygiene regulations
- Gathered guest feedback and recommended improvements
  Notable achievements:
  - Researched new wholesale food suppliers for lower costs while preserving high quality, saving the business nearly 2% per year

Server   2013–2015
Waffle Saloon, Gary, Indiana
- Served food and beverage orders to guests in a 24-table, family-owned, casual dine-in restaurant specializing in breakfast and lunch
- Explained menu offerings to guests and recommended specials and promotions
- Partnered with other servers to ensure all guests' needs were fulfilled
- Performed opening and closing duties, including cleaning dining area, filling condiment containers and sanitizing menus

Hostess   2012–2013
Waffle Saloon, Gary, Indiana
- Welcomed guests, engaged in friendly conversation, suggested new menu items and pointed out special promotions
- Processed payments and made correct change
- Helped with beverage orders for guests
- Completed side work, cleaned and assisted other team members as needed

EDUCATION

Associate of Arts (A.A.) degree, Culinary Arts and Restaurant Management, 2016
Pennsylvania Culinary Institute, Pittsburgh, Pennsylvania

CERTIFICATIONS

ServSafe Manager Certification, 2017
Unrestricted Bartending Permit, Indiana Alcohol & Tobacco Commission, 2014
ServSafe Handler Certification, 2014
Certified Server, Indiana Alcohol & Tobacco Commission, 2014

COMPUTER SKILLS

Google Drive, Microsoft Excel, Microsoft Word, restaurant management software (OpenTable, PeachWorks, Toast), social media (Facebook, Instagram, Twitter)

Morgan L. Bloom
Social Media Coordinator

100 Main Street | South Bend, Indiana 46601 | 574-555-1234 | MorganLaneBloom@gmail.com
LinkedIn.com/in/morganlanebloom

HIGHLIGHTS

- 3 years of social media coordination and content experience
- Bachelor of Science (B.S.) degree in Information Technology
- Advanced knowledge of popular social media platforms, including Facebook, Instagram, LinkedIn, TikTok, Twitter, WhatsApp and YouTube
- Skilled in SEO, design, content management, email management and other related software programs, such as Adobe InDesign, Adobe Photoshop, ConstantContact, Google Analytics and WordPress
- Created and implemented 19 successful social media campaigns for 7 businesses that resulted in higher click-through rates (CTR), lead conversions and organic followers

SOCIAL MEDIA COORDINATION EXPERIENCE

Freelance Social Media Coordinator 2018-Current
South Bend, Indiana

- Develop, pitch, create, execute and track cross-functional social media marketing campaigns for 6 small, independently-owned businesses that include restaurants, online clothing retailers and an organic skincare product line
- Work hand-in-hand with clients to develop long-term social media goals as well as unique, creative and effective social media strategies
- Incorporate search engine optimization (SEO), search engine marketing (SEM), brand messaging and current social media trends
- Measure performance with web analytics tools and key performance indicators (KPIs), including audience growth, reach, engagement, response rate and customer feedback, to measure return on investment (ROI) and campaign effectiveness
- Cultivate relationships with industry-specific social media influencers and direct content with them
- Use social media and email marketing programs (including Agorapulse, Bronto and Planoly) to coordinate, schedule and manage campaigns
- Take photos, set up video shoots and create graphics using Adobe Photoshop and Sketch to produce social media-optimized content for all channels
  Notable achievements:
    - Increased organic impressions 22%, interactions 21% and followers 18% on Instagram for Berber's Café within 60 days
    - Raised CTR 14% for AlisSkinOrganics.com and 12% for Hot Stone Pizzeria within 60 days
    - Improved lead conversions 17% within 60 days for Rewind Clothing and 15% for Paramount Apparel

Assistant Social Media Coordinator/Content Creator 2017–2018
Act-Up Coffee, South Bend, Indiana
- Assisted Social Media Coordinator with creating and managing social media campaigns for a mid-sized coffee bean producer that was seeking to raise its public profile and customer base to attract new investors
- Brainstormed with the CEO and marketing team to develop innovative messaging that aligned with the company's goals and mission statement
- Incorporated SEO, SEM and current social media trends
- Shot photos, set up video shoots and created graphics using Adobe Photoshop and Sketch to produce social media-optimized content for all channels
   Notable achievements:
    - Pitched and successfully implemented an innovative social media campaign on Instagram highlighting the coffee producer's commitment to sustainably-sourced beans and fair wages that was featured on 2 local TV news programs
    - Increased organic impressions 25% and followers 21% within 45 days

Online Marketing Content Intern 2016
South Bend Public Library, South Bend, Indiana
- Selected among 380 applicants for a 16-week internship at the main branch of the South Bend Public Library System
- Assisted the Online Marketing Content Manager with creating and managing social media campaigns on Facebook and Instagram highlighting classes, tutoring and computer services provided by the South Bend Library System

EDUCATION

Bachelor of Science, Information Technology, 2017
Indiana State University

COMPUTER SKILLS

Adobe InDesign, Adobe Photoshop, content management systems (Joomla, Drupal, WordPress), email management programs (Bronto, ConstantContact), G Suite (Google Analytics, Google Drive, Google My Business, Google Shopping), HubSpot, MS Office applications (Word, Excel, Power Point), social media platforms (Facebook, Instagram, LinkedIn, TikTok, Twitter, WhatsApp, YouTube), Sketch

VOLUNTEER POSITIONS

Adoption Marketing Assistant 2018-Present
Paws Patrol Rescue, South Bend, Indiana
- Shoot photos and write playful, engaging biographies of cats, dogs and other domestic pets available for adoption
- Assist in planning adoption events inside PetSmart stores 4 times per year, including coordinating with store managers, recruiting volunteers and designing signage

Parker G. Neelam
Licensed Practical Nurse (L.P.N.)

100 Main Street | South Bend, Indiana 46601 | 574-555-1234 | ParkerGNeelam@gmail.com
Linkedin.com/in/parkergneelam

HIGHLIGHTS

- Licensed Practical Nurse (L.P.N.), State of Indiana Department of Health, issued July 2020
- Certified in Cardiopulmonary Resuscitation (C.P.R.) and Basic Life Support (B.L.S.) from the American Heart Association
- 4 months volunteering in a long-term senior care environment
- 5 years as an administrative assistant, providing a wide range of support to supervisors, organizing events and coordinating communication between multiple departments

PROFESSIONAL EXPERIENCE

Volunteer Senior Aide — 2020-Current
Wide Horizons Care & Rehabilitation, Indianapolis, Indiana
- Visit 4 senior adults weekly at a long-term care facility for 58 elderly, chronically ill, disabled and/or convalescent patients
- Provide companionship and assist with tasks, such as writing letters and engaging in facility activities
- Document patients' general demeanor, physical abilities and health concerns, then submit report to the supervising R.N.

Retail Sales Associate — 2018–Current
Great Lion Groceries, Indianapolis, Indiana
- Provide sales support as a part-time cashier and stocking clerk at a large, family-owned supermarket
- Complete sales and refunds for customers and assist with troubleshooting
- Greet customers, answer questions and alert them to sales and specials
- Clean and sanitize cashier areas, shopping carts and other commonly-touched surfaces
- Maintain full supply of stock on shelves and replenish food service supply station, such as straws, napkins and cup lids

Administrative Assistant — 2013–2018
Miller Media Group, South Bend, Indiana
- Provided administrative support to the Director of Programming at a fast-paced cable network specializing in sporting events and sports news
- Coordinated travel and scheduled in-person and live video meetings
- Acted as liaison between the Director of Programming and other departments

- Logged calls and emails from the public related to programming content and generated reports detailing overall trends in public opinion on current shows
- Accompanied the Director of Programming to live sporting and publicity events
- Maintained records of office and travel expenses for reimbursement
- Ordered supplies and equipment

EDUCATION

Associate of Science, Nursing, June 2020
Ivy Tech Community College, Indianapolis, Indiana

LICENSES AND CERTIFICATIONS

Licensed Practical Nurse (L.P.N.), State of Indiana Department of Health
Issued July 2020, expires July 2021

Cardiopulmonary Resuscitation (C.P.R.) Certification from the American Heart Association

Basic Life Support (B.L.S.) Certification from the American Heart Association

COMPUTER SKILLS

Microsoft Excel, Microsoft Word

Cover Letter Examples

To view PDF versions of these cover letter examples, visit GabrielleLichterman.com/DIYTemplates

Jamie M. Williams
Restaurant Manager

100 Main Street | South Bend, Indiana 46601 | 574-555-1234 | JamieMWilliams@gmail.com
LinkedIn.com/in/jamiemorganwilliams

January 1, 2021

Brenda Bixby
Owner
Café Tarente
101 Main Street
South Bend, Indiana 46601
Via Online Submission

Dear Ms. Bixby:

As soon as I learned of the opening for Restaurant Manager at Café Tarente, I knew I had to submit my application right away. My seven years of restaurant experience, including one year as Manager and two years as Assistant Manager overseeing both F.O.H. and B.O.H. operations, make me the perfect fit for this position. And, as a longtime fan of Café Tarente (I loved the recent addition of "Family-Style" meals to your menu!), this would be my dream job. Let me explain...
    I started my career in the hospitality field as a hostess at the Waffle Saloon—a small, 24-table, family-owned restaurant. It was just a way for me to make a little extra pocket money during high school, however, I discovered a passion for helping customers feel at home while enjoying their favorite comfort foods. It was like being one of the family and welcoming everyone to our breakfast table!
    Inspired by my passion for restaurant hospitality, I left that job to earn my Associate of Arts degree in Culinary Arts and Restaurant Management from the Pennsylvania Culinary Institute. When I returned to Indiana, I became the Assistant Manager, then Manager, at the historic Red Rock Inn. While I have thoroughly enjoyed my time there, I miss the warm, intimate atmosphere of a small eatery. So, I was thrilled to learn you were looking for a Manager at Café Tarente where I've dined many times.
    With my seven years of experience, culinary and restaurant management education, ServSafe certification, Indiana state bartending permit and extensive knowledge of restaurant management platforms, I feel I could hit the ground running and start making a positive impact at Café Tarente right away.
    If you agree and would like to learn more about me, I'd welcome the opportunity to meet for an interview. You can reach me at 574-555-1234 or by emailing me at JamieMWilliams@gmail.com.
    Thank you for your time. I look forward to hearing from you.

Sincerely,
Jamie M. Williams

Morgan L. Bloom
Social Media Coordinator

100 Main Street | South Bend, Indiana 46601 | 574-555-1234 | MorganLaneBloom@gmail.com
LinkedIn.com/in/morganlanebloom

January 1, 2021

Patricia Smith
Human Resources
Four Score Marketing
101 1st Avenue, Suite D
South Bend, Indiana 46601
Via Online Submission

Dear Ms. Smith:

When I spotted the job posting for a Social Media Coordinator on Four Score Marketing's website, I knew I had to reach out. You probably have a wide range of candidates from which to choose. And, like me, they may have the Bachelor of Science degree in Information Technology and at least three years of social media coordinating experience you're seeking. However, my unique background in online content marketing is what sets me apart. Let me explain...

Since the age of 17, I've been creating social media campaigns for clients in the retail and restaurant industries. It all started when my Aunt Eunice asked me to help expand the social media presence of her floral shop, BloomBlooms.com. Even though I had no experience, my aunt promised to pay me with her famous homemade chocolate fudge—so I had plenty of motivation to try.

I quickly learned the fundamentals, including managing social media platforms, search engine optimization and key performance indicators. Within six weeks of launching her first campaign on Instagram, my aunt had a 13% increase in click-throughs to her website and 22% more organic followers on social media. Within 12 weeks, her online flower orders increased 17%. After seeing the powerful effect social media campaigns had for Aunt Eunice's business, I was hooked.

I switched my college major at Indiana State University from English to Information Technology, beat out 379 applicants for a highly-coveted online marketing content internship at the South Bend Public Library System, and was then hired as an Assistant Social Media Coordinator/Content Creator right out school—all while also honing my marketing, photography and graphics skills.

Since 2018, I've been working on a freelance basis, helping six companies grow with fresh, innovative and effective social media content. However, I miss the energy, synergy and camaraderie that comes from working as a member of team. So, I was thrilled to discover that Four Score Marketing was looking for a new Social Media Coordinator. I've been a longtime fan of your campaigns—from the Toboggan Season Instagram challenge and Lavender Mist TikTok aromatherapy competition to the Missy's Cakes memes and Healthwise "Nudge News" content. I admire the out-of-the-box thinking your company is known for. And, I know that I share the same inventive spirit that would allow me to start contributing immediately with your next campaigns.

If you'd like to learn more about me and the kind of creativity and social media know-how I can bring to Four Score, I'd welcome the opportunity to schedule an interview. You can reach me at (574) 555-1234 or MorganLaneBloom@gmail.com.

Thank you for your time. I look forward to hearing from you.

Sincerely,
Morgan L. Bloom

Parker G. Neelam
Licensed Practical Nurse (L.P.N.)

100 Main Street | South Bend, Indiana 46601 | 574-555-1234 | ParkerGNeelam@gmail.com
Linkedin.com/in/parkergneelam

July 15, 2020

Rayna Vasquez
Human Resources
Woodbridge Rehabilitation and Care
200 1st Avenue
South Bend, Indiana 46601
Rayna.Vasqez@WoodbridgeRehabCare.com

Dear Ms. Vasquez:

When I learned that Woodbridge Rehabilitation and Care was seeking a Licensed Practical Nurse from the company's online job board, I knew immediately I had to apply. That's because I'm a recent Nursing graduate and L.P.N. who made a major career change to devote myself to the healthcare field—and to specifically help older adults like those cared for at your facility. Let me explain...

In the summer of 2014, my wonderful grandmother, Sylvia, came to live with my family while she battled breast cancer. As I assisted her with her daily tasks, bathing and medications, I discovered what a joy and privilege it is to aid older generations—and I realized I had a deep passion to do this for others.

So, once my grandmother fully recovered and returned to her own home, I moved to Indianapolis and enrolled in Ivy Tech Community College to obtain my Associate of Science degree in Nursing. Now that I've graduated and have been certified as a Licensed Practical Nurse, I'm ready to move back home to South Bend where I hope to use my nursing skills to help more senior adults live a fuller, happier life—and, of course, to spend more time with my grandmother.

Having grown up in South Bend, I'm familiar with the long tradition of dedicated and individualized treatment that Woodbridge Rehabilitation and Care is known for. It would be an honor to join the nursing team to help continue your mission.

While I am new to nursing, I have worked five years as an administrative assistant, providing a wide variety of support in a fast-paced setting. This gives me the advantage of being ready to assist the R.N.s, doctors and other medical staff with the many tasks involved in quality patient care.

If you'd like to learn more about me by arranging for an interview, please call me at 574-555-1234 or email me at ParkerGNeelam@gmail.com.

Thank you for your time. I look forward to hearing from you.

Sincerely,
Parker G. Neelam

Troubleshooting the Editable, Preformatted Word Document

Did you delete a bulleted list and don't know how to add bullets? With the document open in Microsoft Word:

- Tap to the "Home" tab
- Go to the "Paragraph" editing section on the top ribbon
- Place your cursor where you want to put a bulleted list
- Tap the down arrow on the first icon (which is a bulleted list), then select the type of bullet you want (a round bullet is traditional)
- Start typing your list

(*Note:* If you can't see your editing ribbon on the page, find the pointing-up-arrow-in-a-square icon, which is to the immediate right of your profile photo on the upper right of your page. The icon will display the text "Ribbon Display Options" when you hover your cursor over it. Tap it, then select "Show Tabs and Commands".)

If already wrote a list and need to add bullets after:

- Select the text you want to turn into a bulleted list with your cursor and left mouse button
- Tap the down arrow of the bulleted list icon
- Select the type of bullet you want
- The bullets will automatically appear

If your bullets aren't displaying on each line:

- Place your cursor in front of the first letter of the line where you want a bullet to appear
- Tap "Backspace" until it connects with the line above
- Tap "Enter"
- The bullet will automatically appear

Did your right or left page margins get messed up? With the document open in Microsoft Word:

- Select the text where you need to fix the margins by using your cursor and left mouse button
- For the left margin, use your cursor to move the hourglass-shaped icon on the top ruler to the right or left
- For the right margin, use your cursor to move the half-hourglass icon on the top ruler to the left or right

(*Note:* If you can't see your ruler on your page, tap "View" on the top menu, then in the "Show" section, tap "Ruler" to make a checkmark. The ruler will then show up on your page.)

About Gabrielle Lichterman

Gabrielle Lichterman is an award-winning journalist who has written a weekly personal finance column for *Woman's World* magazine in the U.S. for more than 12 years. Her articles have also appeared in dozens of other major publications, including *First for Women*, *Glamour*, *Marie Claire*, *New York Daily News*, *Self* and *Working Mother*.

    Gabrielle has reported extensively on trends and research in résumés, cover letters and job interviews, surveys of hiring managers and emerging job-seeking technology.

    She has also been a professional writer of résumés and cover letters for more than 20 years. Her clients have spanned a wide spectrum of fields, including accountants, consultants, editors, graphic designers, healthcare professionals, insurance specialists, managers, social media coordinators, teachers, television sportscasters and website developers.

    In addition to her personal finance reporting, Gabrielle is a widely respected women's health journalist and author who penned the award-winning book, *28 Days: What Your Cycle Reveals About Your Moods, Health & Potential*.

    You can learn more at GabrielleLichterman.com.

More Information

To request a consultation or provide feedback about this DIY Résumé and Cover Letter Kit, please contact:

Gabrielle Lichterman at
Gabrielle@GabrielleLichterman.com

Made in the USA
Columbia, SC
28 June 2021